The Hungarian Revolution 1956

Erwin A Schmidl & László Ritter · Illustrated by Peter Dennis

Consultant editor Martin Windrow

First published in Great Britain in 2006 by Osprey Publishing,
Midland House, West Way, Botley, Oxford OX2 0PH, UK
443 Park Avenue South, New York, NY 10016, USA

Email: **info@ospreypublishing.com**

ISBN-10: 1 84603 079 X
ISBN-13: 978 1 84603 079 6

Editor: Martin Windrow
Page layouts by Ken Vail Graphic Design, Cambridge, UK
Typeset in Helvetica Neue and ITC New Baskerville
Index by Alison Worthington
Originated by PPS Grasmere, Leeds, UK
Printed in China through World Print Ltd.

06 07 08 09 10   10 9 8 7 6 5 4 3 2 1

A CIP catalogue record for this book is available from the British Library

FOR A CATALOGUE OF ALL BOOKS PUBLISHED BY
OSPREY MILITARY AND AVIATION PLEASE CONTACT:

North America:
Osprey Direct
C/o Random House Distribution Center, 400 Hahn Road,
Westminster, MD 21157, USA
Email: **info@ospreydirect.com**

All other regions:
Osprey Direct UK
PO Box 140, Wellingborough, Northants, NN8 2FA, UK
Email: **info@ospreydirect.co.uk**

Buy online at **www.ospreypublishing.com**

FRONT COVER COURTESY OF THE
HUNGARIAN NATIONAL MUSEUM

Acknowledgements

PUBLISHED WITH THE CO-OPERATION OF THE
HUNGARIAN INSTITUTE & MUSEUM OF MILITARY HISTORY

This book would not have been possible without the help of
many friends and colleagues, both in Hungary and elsewhere:
At the Hungarian Institute & Museum of Military History,
Budapest, Gen József Holló, Prof László Veszprémy, Tamás
Baczoni, György Ságváry, Peter Illésfalvi and Péter Pap were
so helpful that many of them could with justice be named as
co-authors; this study owes much to their personal efforts.
Special thanks must be given to the Historical Archives of
Hungarian State Security, the Hungarian National Museum,
the Hungarian Police Museum and the Hungarian News
Agency. In particular we wish to acknowledge the help of
Katalin Bognár, György Gyarmati, Mrs Béla Sarnyai and
Zoltán Szántó. Csaba Bekes, László Borhi, László Nagy,
Zoltán Néneth, László Varga, Kristián Ungváry and Col József
Zachar were as helpful as always; and János M.Rainer of the
1956 Institute read and corrected large parts of the draft text.
Ferenc Glatz, Director of the Institute of History of the
Hungarian Academy of Sciences, aided the project
throughout. Iboyla Murber contributed significantly to the
earlier chapters; Edda Engelke, Andreas Gémes, Prof Horst
Haselsteiner, Hofrat Rudolf Hecht, Georg Kastner, Willy
Kerschbaum, Hermine Prügger and Felix Schneider helped
in many ways. Prof István Deák (New York), Frank 'Mick'
Schubert (Alexandria & Győr) and Gabor Boritt (Gettysburg)
made invaluable contributions. We are also indebted to
Capt (Navy, rtd) Prof Valeri Vartanov (Moscow).

Particular thanks are due to Prof Erich Lessing and his
staff, who made possible the use of some of his fascinating
photographs. We also thank Lázslo Sebők, whose maps and
patience exceeded what any author has a right to expect.
Martin Windrow and his colleagues at Osprey Publishing were
most helpful and understanding. And we apologize to anyone
whom we may inadvertently have failed to name.

Above all, we are both grateful to our families for their
patient tolerance while we were writing this study.

Photo Credits

Austrian Army Collection (HBF), Vienna; Getty Images/Hulton
Archive; Hungarian Military Museum & Institute, Budapest;
Hungarian National Museum, Budapest; Hungarian News
Agency (MTI), Budapest; Historical Archives of the Hungarian
State Security (ABTL), Budapest; Erich Lessing Archives,
Vienna; Police Headquarters Burgenland, Eisenstadt; Erwin
A.Schmidl, Vienna; Prof Valeri Vartanov, Moscow.

Artist's Note

Readers may care to note that the original paintings from
which the colour plates in this book were prepared are
available for private sale. All reproduction copyright
whatsoever is retained by the Publishers. All enquiries
should be addressed to:

Peter Dennis,
Fieldhead, The Park, Mansfield, Notts NG18 2AT, UK

The Publishers regret that they can enter into no
correspondence upon this matter.

THE HUNGARIAN REVOLUTION 1956

INTRODUCTION

A small boy rings the doorbell of a house, and an old lady opens the door. 'What do you want, little one?', she asks. Small boy: 'May I come in, please?' Old lady: 'Come in, little boy, but wipe your feet properly.' The boy wipes his feet, enters, and asks: 'Lady, please may I shoot from your window?' *(Hungarian joke, 1956).*

* * *

Budapest is certainly one of Europe's most elegant capitals, recovering today from decades of neglect under Communist rule. To the visitor it is hard to believe that this beautiful city was, half a century ago, one of the 'hot spots' of the Cold War. In 1956 the bloody fighting in the streets of Budapest and of other cities captured the attention of the world. Some 3,000 Hungarians and 720 Soviet soldiers were killed, and nearly 200,000 Hungarians (from a population of some ten million) fled the country to seek new lives elsewhere. This short book hopes to give an overview of the events of 1956, their background and consequences, concentrating on the military aspects.

Historical background

Hungary traces its heritage back to the conquests of the semi-nomadic Magyar tribes who emerged from the Eurasian steppe in the 9th century AD, later becoming Christian and settling in Central Europe. Founded by (Saint) King Stephen at the turn of the first millennium, the Hungarian kingdom became a major power, reaching its zenith in the second half of the 15th century during the reign of the Renaissance monarch Matthias Corvinus. Linked to the Austrian Habsburgs since 1526, most of the country was actually under Ottoman rule for two centuries until the reconquest of the 1680s and 1690s. Following the Ottoman defeat at Vienna in 1683, the twin cities of Buda and Pest were liberated in 1686; most of the country was reunified, and came under Habsburg rule.

After taking over the Budapest Party headquarters on 30 October, insurgents burn posters of the hated Stalinist leader Mátyás Rákosi. One has acquired a Hungarian Army infantryman's greatcoat and a PPSh-41 sub-machine gun. (Lessing Collection No.56-09-10/27)

Rule from Vienna was not always welcome, and there were recurrent periods of tension, culminating in the 'Lawful Revolution' (the title of István Deák's authoritative study) of 1848. This revolution, led by Lajos Kossuth, was crushed by the Habsburgs with the help of Russian forces in 1849; but aspirations for an independent Hungary eventually led to the agreement of 1867 which established the Dual Monarchy. From 1867, Austria and Hungary were linked only by the Habsburg dynasty and by common ministries for foreign affairs, war and finance. Francis Joseph (r.1848–1916) and Charles (1916–18) were both simultaneously Emperor of Austria and King of Hungary. The late 19th century brought unparalleled economic and cultural development; but defeat in World War I resulted not only in the disintegration of the Dual Monarchy but also the dismembering of Hungary, which had reached from the Adriatic Sea to what now is western Ukraine[1]. The Paris peace treaties of 1919–20 (the Trianon treaty of 4 June 1920 was Hungary's equivalent of Germany's Versailles) reduced Hungary to a small state; it lost not only territories populated by other peoples (Slovaks, Serbs, Croats, Romanians and Germans), but also those inhabited by some 3.3 million (or 36 per cent) of ethnic Magyars.

Following the brief but cruel interlude of Béla Kun's Bolshevik dictatorship in 1919, and the ensuing 'White Terror' which was perhaps even worse, Hungary was ruled by Miklós Horthy, a former Austro-Hungarian admiral acting as regent. It was thus a kingdom without a king (after two failed attempts to regain the throne, Emperor-King Charles lived in exile in Madeira, where he died in 1922), ruled by an admiral without a navy (if we discount the Danube flotilla). Economically, all the former Austro-Hungarian territories suffered from relatively slow modernization.

Horthy established a conservative, right-wing, but still parliamentary system. Seeking a revision of the unjust 1920 treaty, he soon sided with the emerging fascist regimes in Italy and Germany, but tried to avoid too close an association for as long as possible. In 1939, Hungary allowed nearly 100,000 Poles, including some 35,000 soldiers, to cross its territory on their way to the West following the occupation of their country by German and Soviet forces.

In the Vienna settlements of 1938–40, Hungary regained part of the territories lost in 1920, notably southern Slovakia, and northern Transylvania from Romania. In 1941, Hungary first served as a base for the German invasion of Yugoslavia (which earned it the return of parts of northern Yugoslavia), and subsequently joined in the German attack on the Soviet Union in June 1941. When the tide of war turned against the Axis, Horthy's prime minister, Miklós Kállay, secretly negotiated an armistice with the Western powers. To prevent Hungary changing sides like Italy, and to ensure the deportation of the last intact Jewish community in Europe, Germany invaded the country on 19 March 1944 and, assisted by Hungary's own fascists (the 'Arrow-Cross' party headed by Ferenc Szálasi), removed the regent from power on 15 October. The implementation of Nazi racial policies in spring 1944 resulted in the deportation and murder of nearly 500,000 Hungarian Jews and 50,000 Roma. Eight months' fierce resistance to the advancing Red Army by

[1] See Osprey Men-at-Arms 392 & 397, *The Austro-Hungarian Forces in World War I, 1914–16 & 1916–18*

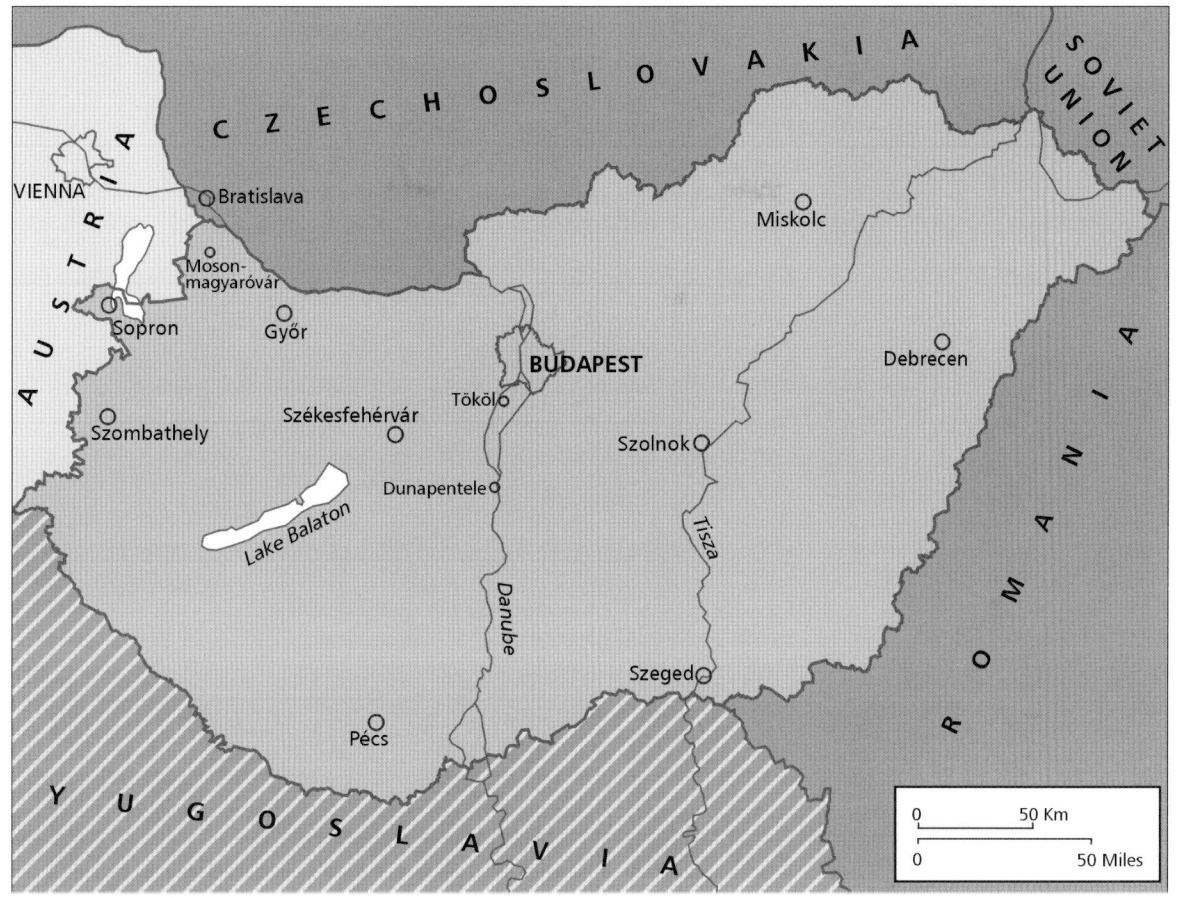

German and Arrow-Cross forces culminated in the 102 day siege of Budapest, which ended on 13 February 1945. The return of peace found the country completely devastated and under Soviet occupation.

Hungary in 1956, with major cities and national frontiers. (Lázslo Sebők)

Hungary after 1945

After World War II, Hungary became part of the Soviet sphere of influence. The new republic was democratic at first, but the presence of the Soviet forces aided the ascendancy of the Communists (although they had gained only 17 per cent of the votes in the November 1945 elections, and 22 per cent in those of 1947). Communist rule was formally established in 1948, and power was concentrated in the hands of Party Secretary General Mátyás Rákosi, one of Stalin's most faithful and at the same time most ambitious followers.

From 1945 some reforms were initiated in an effort to modernize the economy. When the Communists took over and tried to impose a socialist 'workers' and peasants' state' based on the Soviet model, many hoped for significant improvements in living conditions; but due to the inherent contradictions of the system and to mismanagement, the lives of many Hungarians became even harsher. Forced industrialization and the establishment of new 'Socialist towns' led to an unbalanced and stagnant economy. Following the large-scale forced collectivization of agriculture, great numbers of dispossessed ex-farmers drifted to the towns and formed a new 'proletariat'.

Under Rákosi, the Party – officially, the Hungarian Workers' Party (*Magyar Dolgozok Partja*, MDP) – developed into a parallel structure within the state, controlling and regulating the administration.

The education system was brought under strict state control to indoctrinate the next generation. The churches, especially the Catholic Church, became favourite targets of repression; Cardinal József Mindszenty was arrested, and condemned to life imprisonment for 'treason' in 1949. In Budapest, the Regnum Marianum church south-east of Heroes' Square was torn down and a gigantic statue of Stalin erected in its place. Any criticism of the government brought swift and drastic punishment. The main instrument of repression was the State Security Department (*Államvédelmi Osztály*, ÁVO), modelled on the Soviet NKVD and led by Gábor Péter; reorganized in 1950 as the State Security Authority (*Államvédelmi Hatóság*, ÁVH), in 1956 it was still generally known, feared and hated by the original acronym. Between 1947 and 1956 up to 280,000 Hungarians – perhaps one in 40 of the total population – were arrested each year, and close to half of these unfortunates were sentenced for espionage or other 'counter-revolutionary' activities. Among those condemned were even prominent Communists, such as former interior minister László Rajk (who had himself been one of the creators of the ÁVO), and János Kádár, who was to play a crucial role in 1956 and thereafter

First reforms, 1953–56

Following Stalin's death in March 1953, Moscow's course changed markedly. The new Soviet leadership adopted a slightly more moderate policy; this was in part a response to the June 1953 uprisings in East Berlin and strikes in Czechoslovakia, which had been provoked by the deteriorating economic situation under the Communist regimes. In Hungary the standard of living had declined dramatically – from an already low level – since 1951; by 1956 it was lower than it had been in 1938. The forced collectivization campaigns resulted in some of the same hardships as suffered in the USSR in the 1920s–30s – food shortages, reductions in livestock and the depopulation of villages. In June 1953 the Hungarian leadership was summoned to Moscow and sharply criticized. Rákosi had to resign as prime minister, although he remained as first secretary of the Party; his successor as prime minister was Imre Nagy, formerly a cabinet member in 1944–46 and now a junior member of the Politburo.

Nagy took some corrective measures, reviving hopes for economic recovery. Investment in heavy industry was significantly reduced; a new system of compulsory delivery of produce to the state was introduced; it became possible to opt out of the agricultural co-operatives, and there were marked reductions in prices. Nagy also reduced state control of the media, and encouraged discussion within the Party on political and economic reforms. In August 1953 political prisoners serving sentences not exceeding two years were given an amnesty, and internment camps and internal exile were ended. In December 1955, Hungary (together with Austria and 14 other nations) was accepted into the United Nations.

Rákosi continued his activities in the background, however, and in January 1955 Nagy in his turn was summoned to Moscow. He was severely criticized for the radicalism of his reforms, and ordered to correct the mistakes. Exploiting the situation, Rákosi began a campaign within the Party, accusing Nagy of 'rightist deviation'; Nagy was dismissed as prime minister, and later even stripped of his Party membership. Rákosi became prime minister once again and, in response to the hardening of Soviet policy, he repealed Nagy's reforms one after the other during the spring of 1955. But the turmoil within the Soviet world was not over: Nikita S.Khrushchev emerged as the new leader in the Kremlin, and in February 1956 he launched an open attack on Stalin at the 20th Communist Party Congress in Moscow. The Kremlin feared that internal tensions in Hungary could escalate out of control, and Rákosi was finally forced from power that July; he was ordered to Moscow, where he remained until his death in 1971.

OPPOSITE **The infamous Hungarian Communist leader Mátyás Rákosi (centre) visiting troops on manoeuvres, September 1952. Like many of the post-war Stalinist bosses, Rákosi had spent the war years in Moscow; he would later boast of his elimination of the leaders of the non-Communist majority in 1945–48 as like 'cutting off slices of salami'. Despite Stalin's insistence that the USSR's satellite states build up large forces in preparation for resisting a Western attack, Rákosi's handling of the Hungarian People's Army in 1948–56 in fact made it a divided and uncertain instrument for internal repression. The official on the left is Ernő Gerő, then assistant secretary general of the Party, and in 1956 briefly Rákosi's successor. (Hungarian Military Museum)**

Student demonstrators on 23 October 1956; some wear lapel ribbons in the national colours, and note the flag with the Communist motif cut out of the middle – this soon became the symbol of the uprising. (Hungarian Military Museum)

However, it was not Nagy who was re-appointed as Rákosi's successor, but Ernő Gerő. This transparently cosmetic move only fuelled public dissatisfaction; sensing the weakness of the government, ever broader masses of people – from intellectuals to steel workers – dared to confront the leadership, sending clear signals of support for the reformist opposition gathering around Nagy. On 3 October 1956 the Party Central Committee announced that László Rajk and others had wrongly been convicted of treason in 1949, and ten days later Nagy was reinstated as a member of the Party. Following these rehabilitations, many Communist functionaries began to doubt the moral justifications of the Party in which they had believed. After the reburial of Rajk on 6 October, students in Budapest started to shout anti-Communist slogans. Although at first mainly concerned about changes in their curricula, the disgruntled students soon engaged politically. On 16 October, students at Szeged in the south-east formed an independent student union. Not to be outdone, students from the Budapest Technical University joined the Szeged group on 22 October. They no longer wanted reforms, but radical change: their demands included the withdrawal of Soviet troops, the announcement of democratic elections, the reinstatement of national symbols and holidays, and the removal of Stalin's statue from Budapest. To give voice to their demands, and to express sympathy with the concurrent Polish de-Stalinization process, a peaceful march was announced for the next day. (In Poland, security forces had violently put down a strike in Poznan in June 1956; but despite the stationing of Soviet tanks around Warsaw in October, the situation was carefully de-escalated, leading to the installation of a relatively more moderate government under Vladislav Gomulka.)

THE EVENTS OF 1956

The beginning: 23 October

On Tuesday 23 October the country awoke to a warm, summery day. Despite the widespread agitation for reform the political leadership was indecisive: in the morning it banned the student demonstration, but a few hours later unexpectedly granted permission for it to go ahead. Police were ordered not to use force, and members of the Party's Budapest organizations were instructed to take part in the demonstration to prevent it getting out of hand. The demonstration started from the statue of Sándor Petőfi (a hero-poet of the 1848 Revolution) on the Pest (north-eastern) side of the River Danube, then crossed Margit Bridge to the memorial of another hero of 1848, the Polish-born General József Bem; here it met another group coming from the Technical University. On the way the numbers of demonstrators were swelled by workers on their way home from the morning shift.

Intoxicated by its own size and courage, the crowd began to chant more and more radical slogans: 'Down with Gerő!'; 'Nagy into the government, Rákosi into the Danube!'; 'Russians go home!' At Bem's statue more and more Hungarian flags appeared, with the Soviet-style Communist coat-of-arms (the so-called 'Rákosi badge') cut out; the national flags with the hole in the middle instantly became the symbol of the nascent revolution.

By late afternoon the crowd had swollen, by some accounts to 200,000 people. A large group marched to the Parliament building, demanding that Imre Nagy speak to them. It was several hours before he appeared; this might have been a last chance for a trusted leader to take control of a situation that was increasingly spinning out of control. However, Nagy caused huge disappointment, urging that conflicts be resolved within the Party, and appealing to the crowd to disperse. This fanned rather than dampened the tension.

At the same time as Nagy was speaking, a crowd on Dózsa György Road close to the City Park toppled the statue of Stalin, the symbol of the system, with the aid of cutting torches; its fall seemed to symbolize the fall of Communist rule in Hungary. The eight-metre high bronze colossus was dragged by lorry to Blaha Lujza Square and cut into pieces for souvenirs. (A part of one hand is on display in the National Museum in Budapest, while other fragments travelled as far as Texas.) The head of the statue remained lying in the street for days, with a 'no through road' sign rammed up its nose.

A third group of demonstrators gathered in Bródy Sándor Street at the Hungarian Radio building, with the intent of broadcasting the demands drawn up by the students the previous night. The station management did not permit this, however, airing instead Gerő's speech in which he described the protesters as 'nationalist provocateurs'. This speech was intended not so much to intimidate the public as to motivate

Among the Soviet tanks that moved into Budapest on 24 October were some of the latest T-54s, seen here at the corner of Dohány utca and Erzsébet Körút. Although they were under strict orders not to fire unless fired upon, their intervention inevitably turned an internal confrontation between Hungarians and their government into a nationalist uprising. (Hungarian Military Museum)

the uncertain police, military and Party apparatus; but predictably, it only added fuel to the flames. The impatient and swelling crowd began to stone the building. At some time after 9pm, feeling threatened, ÁVH guards opened fire, leaving many dead and wounded in the street. The crowd did not back down even in the face of this ultimate threat; and some of them – including workers from arms factories and warehouses – set off to obtain weapons. Others armed themselves from a load of weapons that had been concealed in two ambulances in an attempt to smuggle them into the radio station. Soon the crowd started to return the fire of the secret police. The true turning point came when soldiers from the Hungarian Army's 8th Tank Regiment, arriving to reinforce the defence of the radio station, decided to join the demonstrators instead, and also came under fire from the ÁVH guards. The soldiers distributed weapons and ammunition to the demonstrators, and joined in the siege of the building.

Soon the news had spread across the whole city that the State Security had fired on unarmed demonstrators at the radio station, and the crowds reacted with uncontrollable fury. Cars and trams were overturned and set alight; demonstrators spread out in search of weapons, chanting 'Death to the ÁVH! Let's get weapons!' Before long a large quantity of small arms had been obtained from police stations – where many policemen sided with the insurgents – and the ammunition stores of large factories and the MÖHOSZ (Hungarian Voluntary Defence Association) were soon in the hands of the demonstrators. The armed uprising in Budapest had begun.

A government attempt to retrieve the situation by appointing Imre Nagy as premier, while Gerő remained in control of the Party, came too late.

Major demonstrations also broke out that day in other industrial and university towns. Although the focus was always on Budapest, the first shots were actually fired in Debrecen, in the east of the country, at 6pm that evening, where three demonstrators killed when the ÁVH opened fire became the first casualties of the Revolution.

First Soviet intervention: 24–28 October

Soviet forces had been stationed in Hungary since 1945. Following Hungary's signing of a peace treaty with the Allies in 1947, they stayed under the pretext of guarding the supply lines for Soviet troops in Austria, which remained under quadripartite Allied occupation. When this ended with the Vienna State Treaty of 15 May 1955, and Austria adopted a formal but pro-Western policy of neutrality between the two blocs, many Hungarians saw this as a model for their own country; but the Soviets were there to stay. A day before the signing of the Vienna Treaty the Warsaw Pact was signed, forming the basis for the continued stationing of Soviet forces in Hungary. Soviet troops were moved from Austria to Hungary, where they were reorganized as a 'Special Corps' under direct control from Moscow. The Hungarians' hope that Khrushchev's policy of de-Stalinization would include the granting of more independence from the Soviet Union was to prove vain.

On the late afternoon of 23 October 1956, Party secretary Gerő asked the Soviet Union for assistance; this appeal was prompted by the

In the early stages of the uprising Hungarians tried to start discussions with Soviet soldiers, to explain that they were not 'fascist counter-revolutionaries' but workers and students. Usually the soldiers showed no hostility, and some even swapped caps with the demonstrators. This soldier wears a *pilotka* cap and a khaki canvas 'working jacket' over his uniform instead of the cumbersome greatcoat; note also the AK-47 assault rifle. (MTI Budapest, No.GP1956 1030018)

escalation of the uprising, and the fact that Hungarian officers and soldiers – many of whom were on leave because of a major army reorganization that was then under way – were joining the demonstrators. Gerő was supported by the Soviet ambassador, Yuri V. Andropov (who would become head of the KGB in 1967–82, and Party secretary general in 1982–84). According to later reports, Soviet military commanders in Budapest advised against the involvement of Soviet troops, rightly arguing that Soviet intervention would only stiffen the demonstrators' resolve. Khrushchev himself had hoped for a peaceful settlement on the Polish model, and was hesitant to endanger the international détente of the day; but, following the demands from Budapest, he agreed at a Central Committee meeting shortly before midnight – 9pm Budapest time – to instruct units of the Special Corps to intervene to restore law and order. (However, the written request for intervention from the Hungarian government which Khrushchev demanded was only delivered on 28 October.)

Soviet garrisons were alerted on the evening of 23 October, following a plan first drawn up in the summer of 1956. Soviet as well as Hungarian tanks entered the city at dawn on 24 October; their commanders hoped that a show of force would be sufficient to quell the uprising, but they misjudged the Hungarians. They came up against stiff resistance; local

On 25 October crowds gathered in front of the Parliament building, fraternizing with Soviet tank crews, and even clambering on to the tanks waving Hungarian flags (here with the old pre-Communist coat-of-arms). When shots were fired, possibly by Hungarian State Security snipers, this peaceful demonstration turned into a bloodbath. (Hungarian Military Museum)

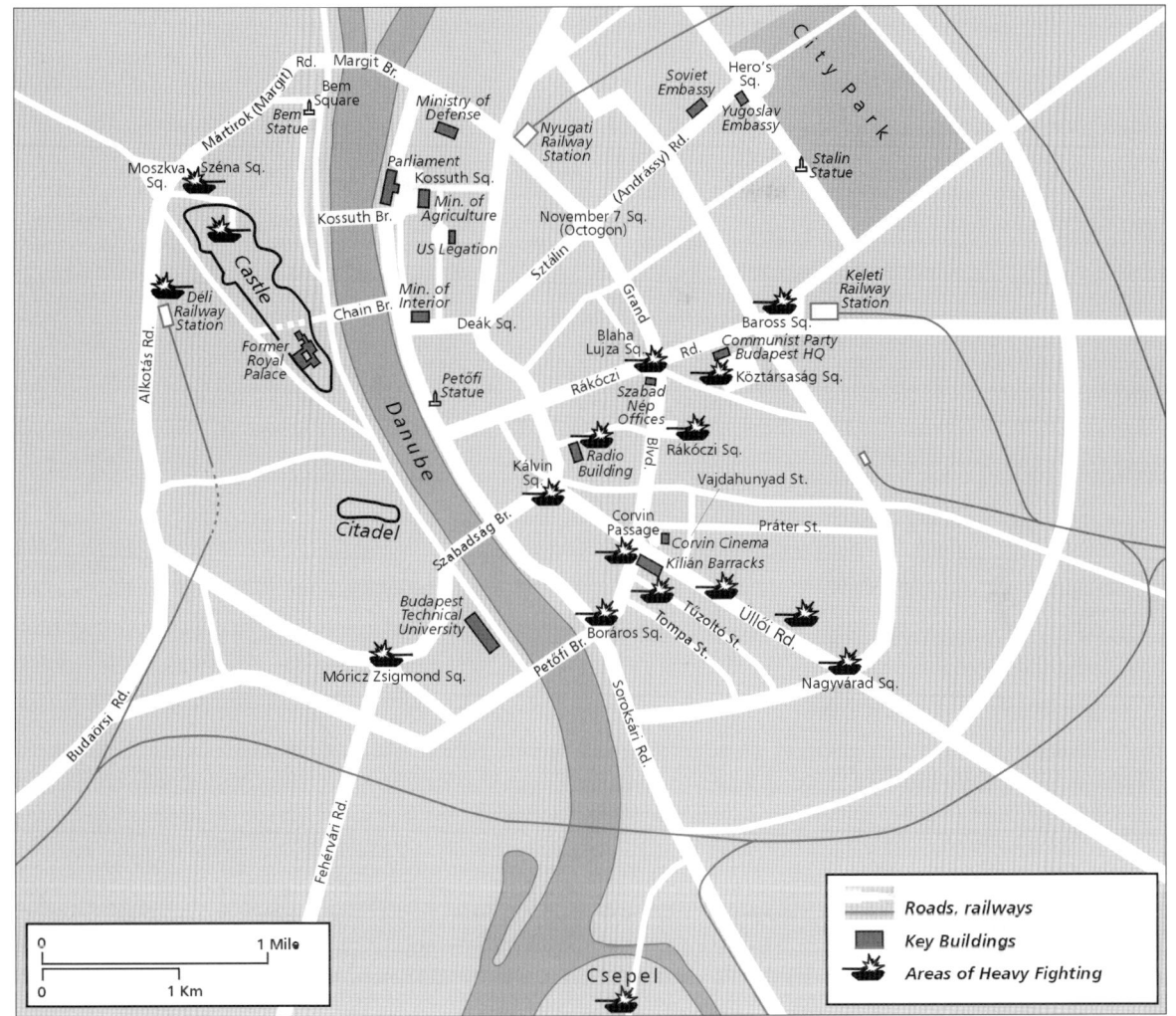

insurgent groups controlled crucial traffic chokepoints, and managed to hold the unprepared Soviet troops at bay. The first units of the Special Corps' 2nd Guards Mechanized Division were greeted with roadblocks and heavy gunfire; tanks with overheating engines, and open-topped armoured personnel carriers, proved vulnerable to 'Molotov cocktails' – improvised fire-bombs – thrown from windows above.

Although the Soviets managed to take control of the Parliament building, the ministries, the bridges and the railway stations, a number of vital points in the city remained firmly in the insurgents' hands. With just 700 soldiers and 50 tanks initially available, there was no chance of securing the 40 or 50 most important objectives. Confusion and insecurity reigned, and it took the reconnaissance units some time to assess the situation in Budapest. On 24 October alone more than 20 Soviet soldiers were killed in the fighting. Not only were the forces available too few, and ill-prepared for action in city streets, but there was also too little communication and co-operation with the Hungarian forces or Police who could have provided crucial local knowledge. As there were no precise orders, the majority of the Hungarian People's Army units deployed in Budapest remained inactive; some units disintegrated almost

Budapest in 1956, with the main locations mentioned in this text. (Lázslo Sebők)

Open-topped Soviet APCs and towed artillery were vulnerable to firing and 'Molotov cocktails' from the higher floors of tall buildings. Note the burnt tyres of this 122mm howitzer from the 33rd Guards Mechanized Division, abandoned on Ferenc Boulevard. (Hungarian Military Museum)

immediately, with individual soldiers or even entire sub-units joining the insurgents. Passivity and confusion also characterized many Police units, and even those of the ÁVH. Sending the Soviets in had predictably inflamed Hungarian nationalist sentiments, and what had begun as a demonstration over internal grievances now escalated into a Hungarian fight against foreign occupiers.

* * *

Despite the presence of Soviet forces in and around Budapest, the uprising continued in the capital as well as in other towns. In centres as far apart as Pécs in the south-west and Miskolc in the north-east, workers' councils and similar ad hoc institutions were formed, usually uniting intellectuals, workers' leaders and some officials, and often including Army officers. The state radio declared on 25 October that the 'attempted counter-revolutionary coup d'état' had been thwarted, and instructed the people of Budapest to go to work. In the face of this obviously false claim, Hungarian Army and Police units remained indecisive, and embarrassed Soviet soldiers clearly did not know who to fight or why. Before long, unarmed crowds surrounded the Soviet tanks, trying to explain in every possible way that they were workers and students and not fascist counter-revolutionaries. In many places they were successful; some Soviet commanders declared that they were not going to shoot, and even allowed the demonstrators to climb on tanks and hoist the Hungarian flag. The growing number of friendly encounters, however, came to an abrupt halt when news spread of a massacre on Kossuth Square.

There, in front of the Parliament building, the crowds were escorted by Soviet tanks covered with demonstrators. Shortly after 11am on 25 October shots were fired, causing panic among both the demonstrators and the Soviet soldiers. The Soviets on the square thought that the demonstrators had led them into a trap, and started shooting: 75 people died and 284 were injured in Kossuth Square and neighbouring streets. Research to date has been unable to confirm who fired the first shots or where they came from; among the possible culprits are an ÁVH detachment watching the square from the rooftops of buildings, or a Soviet tank commander acting on the orders of KGB chief Ivan A.Serov, who wanted to prevent fraternization between the Soviet soldiers and Hungarians at all costs.

The massacre made clear that Gerő's crisis management was unable to stem the tide. Barely an hour after the event, on the initiative of Imre Nagy and the members of the Soviet delegation, Gerő was replaced as first secretary by János Kádár; but again, this did not lead to a lasting solution. Nagy and Kádár only offered inconsequential, weak and long overdue reforms, which were too little to win over the public. News of the events on Kossuth Square spread like wildfire, making the insurgents even more determined and prompting thousands more to take up arms against the Soviets and ÁVH. The series of demonstrations that erupted in provincial towns and cities sent a message that the people were behind the insurgents. This was a decisive moment: for many, the uprising became a national war of independence, and the insurgents became freedom fighters who could depend on the unequivocal, often self-sacrificial support of a significant part of the population right up to the bitter end.

During the first Soviet intervention the area around Corvin Passage became the scene of some of the heaviest fighting. The Soviets lost several tanks and other AFVs there, including these ISU-152 self-propelled howitzers. The hull numbers ('196' and '190') were in dark yellow on the forest-green paint finish. The memoirs of the local insurgent group's leader in November, Gergely Pongrácz, suggest that these were knocked out with a captured 76.2mm anti-tank gun; '196' was later used by the insurgents. (Hungarian National Museum No.69-2303)

While the initial demonstrators had mostly been students and intellectuals, followed by workers, they were now joined by numbers of criminals, some coming directly from the opened jails. This later allowed Soviet propaganda to exaggerate the role played by 'criminal elements'. Despite Soviet allegations to the contrary, however, the whole affair had started spontaneously, and there was almost no involvement by the 'old elites' or from the West. It is also difficult to ascribe a single political motivation to the uprising. Some took up arms against the Communist dictatorship because of their own experiences at the hands of the secret police, or in a spasm of protest against their terrible living conditions. Some wanted a 'reformed Socialist' system based on the Yugoslav model. Some were motivated by nationalist feelings and a yearning for Hungary to be able to decide her future for herself. And some, it has to be said, were notorious troublemakers, fighting authority wherever they could. Frustration with existing conditions turned into outbursts of hate and violence, such as the occasional lynchings of ÁVH and Soviet soldiers, or the looting and burning of two Russian book-shops, *Horizon* and *Szikra*, in Budapest.

There was no general looting, however, and the general strike called on 26 October made it clear that the uprising was supported by large segments of the population, who now increasingly demanded the withdrawal of Soviet troops from Hungary, dissolution of the State Security apparatus, and multi-party democracy. An interesting feature shown in many contemporary photographs are the masses of people

Watched somewhat incredulously by Hungarians, Soviet armour withdraws from Budapest following the ceasefire of 28 November. This shows a T-54 followed by BTR-152 armoured personnel carriers. (Hungarian Military Museum)

in the streets during the fighting: some queuing up for bread, some standing by and watching, and many apparently passing by without taking too much interest in the fighting.

* * *

After new divisions of Soviet troops arrived in Budapest on 25 October, the engagements became fiercer. The 128th Guards Rifle Division from the USSR was deployed in Buda (the south-western side of the river); and the 33rd Guards Mechanized Division from Romania had instructions to flush the insurgents out of the south-eastern quarters of the city. Lacking appropriate reconnaissance and infantry support, the 33rd Div came up against the strongest insurgent groups in the 8th and 9th Districts, particularly around the Corvin Passage. In this area alone the Soviets lost 14 tanks and self-propelled guns, nine other armoured vehicles, 13 artillery pieces, four multiple rocket-launchers, and six anti-aircraft guns over the next three days. Many were destroyed by the insurgents while still in column of march before they could fire a single round.

The Kilián Barracks, on the corner of Üllői Road and Grand Boulevard opposite the Corvin Passage, played a major role in the insurgents' success. Most of the soldiers stationed in the barracks were members of the Military Technical Auxiliary Corps, the labour service branch of the Hungarian People's Army. During the first two days of the Revolution the officers opposed the insurgents; but the rank-and-file not only fraternized with them, but often fought alongside them against

Among the Soviet tanks captured was this PT-76 light amphibian, '711', seen here at Károly Körút with a load of triumphant insurgents wearing typical berets and trench coats. (MTI Budapest, No.BA1956 1024004)

On 30 October, ÁVH personnel fired into a crowd at the Budapest Party headquarters. Six Hungarian T-34/85 tanks were sent in, and (possibly by accident) joined the demonstrators; here one is seen firing into the building, while insurgents take cover behind it. After the crowd stormed the office block they lynched 23 ÁVH men – some disguised in Police uniforms – and left several mutilated bodies hanging from trees. (Hungarian Military Museum)

the Soviets. When the tank officer Col Pál Maléter arrived at the barracks on 25 October, with the approval of more senior officers he agreed a ceasefire with the insurgents in the area that led to a cessation of hostilities between them and the Hungarian Army. At the same time he resisted repeated Soviet attacks, as a result of which Kilián became one of the armed centres of the uprising.

Meanwhile, the demonstrations escalated in the provinces as the Party's power continued to disintegrate rapidly. Serious incidents occurred on 26 October in Mosonmagyaróvár and in Esztergom, where ÁVH and Border Guards felt threatened and fired into demonstrating crowds, killing altogether 67 people. Smaller incidents occurred in Nagykanizsa and in Miskolc; there and in Mosonmagyaróvár, the insurgents subsequently lynched several ÁVH officers. On 27 October, Free Győr Radio began to broadcast; this station would become one of the most important sources of information in the ensuing days.

Only in Kecskemét and its surroundings was the Revolution successfully crushed, by MajGen Lajos Gyurkó, the commander of the Hungarian 3rd Corps. Proclaiming martial law, he threatened to execute any soldier who joined the insurgents. On 27 October he had two MiG-15 fighters strafe a demonstration in Tiszakécske, killing 17 people and injuring 110. It is no surprise that Gyurkó's name was mentioned in Soviet military circles as the only Hungarian military leader capable of putting down the 'counter-revolution'. After the fighting ended on 31 October, Gyurkó and his political deputy fled to the Soviets to escape being held accountable for their actions.

ÁBTL 4.1 A-236

By 28 October it had become clear that the Hungarian leadership had two options: either to accept the proposal of the hardliners and use dependable military and ÁVH units, armed former partisans and reinforced Soviet troops to crush the Revolution; or to take the initiative by a show of willingness to negotiate. The Hungarian government decided on the latter course, to which – if reluctantly – the Soviets also gave their blessing. Military conditions were still against them: the Soviet divisions that had been in combat in the city streets for days were in dire need of rest. The Soviets' last operation, to take Corvin Passage at dawn on the 28th, ended in a fiasco: within half an hour the insurgents thwarted the attack, destroying three T-34s and two T-54s, and this failure contributed significantly to the Soviet agreement to a ceasefire later that day.

While the situation quickly stabilized in most towns under the direction of the new 'revolutionary councils', in Budapest itself some fighting continued, and many armed groups refused to lay down their arms before the complete withdrawal of the Soviets. There was distrust on both sides, and the decentralized nature of the uprising made negotiations difficult; some local leaders who wanted to end the fighting were removed or ignored by their men.

After the ceasefire had been declared, Nagy announced an entirely new government programme in his afternoon radio speech. Instead of a 'counter-revolution', he described the uprising as a 'great national and democratic movement' which had erupted out of the 'grave crimes of the preceding era'. He announced the recognition of the revolutionary organizations, and guaranteed impunity for the insurgents, the disbandment of the ÁVH, and the restitution of national holidays and

In towns throughout the country political and workers' councils took over local authority during the heady days of the last week in October. This photo shows a meeting of such a council; the Hungarian Army officer with his back to the camera wears an armband in national colours to show his allegiance to the Revolution. (Hungarian State Security Archives ÁBTL 4.1, album A-237/ 172)

In many places barricades were erected to slow down Soviet tanks, as here in Lövöház Street near Széna Square, just north of Castle Hill in Buda. (Photo Dr Tibor Szentpétery; Hungarian Military Museum)

the traditional Hungarian coat-of-arms. Based on an agreement with the Soviet government, Soviet troops would immediately start to withdraw from Budapest, and talks on their complete withdrawal from Hungary would begin shortly.

With this radio address the government fell into line with the demands of the 23 October demonstration, and negotiations with the leaders of the insurgent groups could begin. Meanwhile the Soviet troops drew back from Budapest, and the Soviet government made a statement of its intent to respect the sovereignty and territorial integrity of its Warsaw Pact allies. At this moment it appeared that the Revolution had triumphed.

BOTH PAGES **On 3 November, Soviet and Hungarian officers met in the Parliament building to discuss terms for a Soviet withdrawal. The delegations were headed respectively by the Soviet deputy chief of the general staff, Gen M.S.Malinin (third from left); and the newly appointed Hungarian defence minister, MajGen Pál Maléter (right centre – see Plate F2). Malinin wears the blue-green parade version of the double-breasted tunic introduced for general officers in 1954; Maléter wears the Hungarian version, in khaki (there was also a grey parade version for colonels and generals). When the Soviets took part in these talks a military solution had already been decided upon, and within hours Maléter and some of his staff would be arrested. (Hungarian Military Museum)**

Interlude: 29 October–4 November

Slowly, the reformed Nagy government took control. It eventually included representatives of different parties, notably the Smallholders Party, the Social Democratic Party and the Petőfi Peasants Party, which re-emerged as they were legalized, and 'revolutionary councils' took over control in the various counties. However, on 30 October renewed fighting erupted around the Budapest Party headquarters in the 8th District, where jumpy ÁVH personnel fired into a crowd; among those killed were doctors and nurses trying to assist the wounded. Six Hungarian Army tanks were sent in, but their crews sided with the crowds and fired into the building, and the demonstrators eventually gained the upper hand. Twenty-three ÁVH personnel were killed, some of them when they tried to surrender; and some were hung from nearby trees and their corpses mutilated. Western photographers were on hand, and the photographs of these lynchings went around the world; they would later figure prominently in Soviet attempts to justify their final intervention.

Meanwhile, however, workers' councils declared that work would start again on Monday 5 November (in some factories work resumed on Saturday 3rd). Together with the military and a new 'National Guard', the revolutionary councils planned security measures. Soviet forces had withdrawn from Budapest, but troop movements continued throughout the country, and massive reinforcements (notably from the 7th and 31st Guards Airborne Divisions) started to arrive. When Soviet representatives in Budapest tried to explain – not too convincingly – that these movements were just preparations for leaving the country, Nagy eventually declared on 1 November that Hungary intended to withdraw from the Warsaw Pact. Following the Austrian model, Hungary should become neutral, and he asked first the Western powers and then the United Nations to defend Hungary's neutrality and to mediate in the

dispute with the Soviet Union. At the same time, Nagy tried to convince the Soviets that this was not a 'counter-revolution', but a continuation of the Socialist development begun in 1945. He also sought Polish and Yugoslav intercession with Moscow on Hungary's behalf.

Although the decision to intervene by force had already been taken in Moscow on 31 October, at noon on 3 November Hungarian and Soviet officers started negotiations in Parliament about details of the Soviet troop withdrawal. The Hungarian delegation was headed by Col Pál Maléter, the tank officer who had supported the uprising in Budapest, and who had just been promoted major-general and appointed minister of defence. A former Communist partisan, Maléter deliberately put on his old Soviet decorations before the meeting. Later that day, he and other leading officers drove to the Soviet temporary headquarters at Tököl Air Base to continue the negotiations – but when they arrived, they were arrested. Hungary was thus deprived of its top military leadership at the start of the second intervention.

Second Soviet intervention: 4–12 November

For the leadership in Moscow, the situation was difficult to assess. At the beginning of the crisis two senior officials had been sent to Budapest, Deputy Prime Minister Anastas I.Mikoyan and Presidium member Mikhail A.Suslov. The head of the KGB, Gen Ivan A.Serov, was also in Budapest; and from their reports, the Kremlin concluded that a peaceful solution had become impossible, and that armed intervention was necessary to prevent Hungary from drifting any further out of the Communist bloc.

On 31 October, Khrushchev agreed; the new Hungarian Communist Party first secretary, János Kádár, was called to Moscow, and on 2 November he was ordered to form a new government – being handed a list of his new ministers written in Russian, which he could not read. In the meantime, preparations for the second intervention continued. This was to include not only forces from the 8th and 38th Armies from the south-western USSR, but also the 7th and 31st Guards Airborne Divisions from the Caucasus regions, which had already started to fly in on 30 October. Overall commander was the Warsaw Pact C-in-C, Marshal Ivan S.Konev, while MajGen Kuzma E.Grebennik commanded the forces in the Budapest region. At the same time 600 Soviet military families were flown out of Hungary. Apart from the Soviet forces, the Czechoslovak People's Army was also put on alert, and reinforced border troops and garrisons in Slovakia from late October on. There was no deployment of other Warsaw Pact forces on Hungarian soil, however.

* * *

Operation *Vichr* ('Whirlwind') began in the early morning hours of 4 November, when strategic airfields, highway junctions and bridges were secured. Because the Soviets feared resistance by the Hungarian Army, its barracks were among the prime targets. Aided by Hungarian State Security, Soviet troops occupied the Parliament in Budapest, which had become a symbol of the Revolution. In a dramatic radio broadcast at 5.20am, Imre Nagy informed the world of the intervention and appealed for help, before taking refuge in the Yugoslav Embassy. Kádár also broadcast, announcing that the popular movement had deteriorated into a 'fascist' uprising, that he had formed a new government, and that he had asked the Soviet Union to intervene.

The November leader of the Corvin group, Gergely Pongrácz, at his desk in an apartment borrowed from a doctor just behind the cinema (which can be seen through the window). He is apparently wearing an M-51 Army tunic; the man behind him wears a padded jacket. (Lessing Collection No.56-09-07/6A)

The 2nd Guards Mechanized Division occupied the north-eastern and central parts of Budapest, including Parliament and the Danube bridges, while the 33rd Division operated in the south-east. In the west, the 128th Division had to occupy the Castle and the Gellért hills, facing stiff resistance. Usually the Soviet troops operated in small task forces consisting of a company of 100 or 150 soldiers in armoured carriers supported by about a dozen tanks. They soon occupied military installations and disarmed Hungarian military and National Guard units. Local fighting erupted repeatedly, and some pockets of resistance held out for about a week. One of the fiercest points of resistance was the area around the Corvin Cinema, against which massive artillery firepower was assembled. Mortars were also used against some of the workers' quarters, killing over 100 civilians in their apartments.

By 6 November more than 30,000 Soviet troops were in Budapest, and the outcome of the fighting was never in doubt. Responsible Hungarian officers tried to keep their men out of this hopeless battle, while local insurgent groups occasionally continued to resist. Throughout the country, Soviet forces overcame resistance by Army, National Guard and local groups. There were no pitched battles, and Soviet troops usually tried to force the insurgents to retire without getting drawn into close-quarter fighting, unleashing mortars and artillery against stubborn pockets of resistance.

Most resistance ended on 11 November, although sporadic activities – such as the occasional blowing up of railway lines – continued well into the winter. Altogether, some 3,000 Hungarians are thought to have

Following the second Soviet intervention of 4 November, a BTR-152 APC patrols the street next to the National Theatre, while workers start to repair some of the damage. The Soviet soldiers wear greatcoats with *pilotka* and *ushanka* caps. (Lessing Collection No.56-10-10/19)

been killed in the fighting of October and November 1956; the casualties were officially given as 2,502 dead and 19,226 wounded, but the real figures were probably higher. The Soviets counted 720 dead, 1,540 wounded and 51 missing.

Hungary and Suez

There has always been speculation about the concurrence of the two major crises of 1956. Simultaneously with the Hungarian Revolution, Israeli forces invaded the Egyptian Sinai on 30 October with the collusion of Britain and France, who both landed forces in Egypt on 6 November to secure the Suez Canal, which had been nationalized by President Gamal Abdel Nasser on 26 July. This Operation 'Musketeer' failed to achieve its objectives, however; the US openly denounced the Anglo-French operation, the Israelis had to retire to their pre-war borders, and the UN started its first 'blue helmet' peace-keeping operation. From all that is known, both crises and both interventions developed independently of each other. However, international reactions were partially influenced by the two parallel events, and US officials complained that they were hampered by having to deal with two major crises (and the troubles in Poland) at the same time. Obviously, the Anglo-French operation robbed the West of much moral authority in the eyes of the world, and thus weakened the basis for international criticism of the Soviet crushing of the Hungarian Revolution.

Despite the separate development of the two conflicts, some of the Soviet airborne forces were apparently under the impression that they had been sent to Egypt. Eyewitnesses remember being asked by Soviet soldiers whether the river – the Danube – was indeed the Suez Canal (one of those asked was actually a US Special Forces officer in civilian dress, who was able to answer in perfect Russian). Prompted by earlier American rhetoric and broadcasts over Radio Free Europe, many Hungarians had hoped for military intervention by the West. As this would have carried the risk of a major war between the two blocs, including the possible use of nuclear weapons, President Dwight D.Eisenhower clearly excluded this option. When Spanish Generalissimo Franco suggested supporting the Hungarian rising the US vetoed such a plan. The Hungarian issue was brought before the UN General Assembly, however, and was regularly brought up there until 1962.

The refugees

The Hungarian government had started to dismantle part of the 'Iron Curtain' in the spring of 1956, removing some minefields and barbed wire fences. This later made possible the mass exodus of refugees crossing into Austria (and to a lesser extent, Yugoslavia). The first refugees appeared in late October, including Communist Party members and ÁVH agents who feared retribution (though most of these fled to the east).

Help for the Hungarian insurgents came from all over the world; here Red Cross trucks with medical supplies assemble at the Austrian border – note the conspicuous white costume of the Red Cross worker. The uniformed men (centre) are Austrian soldiers and *gendarmes*. The Austrian envoy in Budapest, Walter Peinsipp, organized three medical depots and distributed supplies. Some of these were brought in by Austrian students, and even young Boy Scouts, who travelled all the way to Budapest. In the prevailing anti-Communist mood the boys' absence from school was tolerated, and the 'long weekend' of early November made these trips easier – Thursday 1 and Friday 2 November were school holidays in Austria. (Hungarian Military Museum)

Cadets from one of two 'alarm companies' hastily assembled by the Austrian Military Academy patrol close to the Hungarian border (though not so close as the flags suggest – this is a posed photograph). They wear field-grey greatcoats with red collar patches, and gold cuff stripes to indicate their officer-candidate status; helmets, webbing and weapons are US surplus. Carrying a BAR in the foreground is Cadet (now BrigGen, rtd) Nik Horvath, whose family came from a border area. (Austrian Army/HBF)

In Austria, the initial developments in Hungary were greeted cheerfully, the eastern part of the country having been under ten years of Soviet occupation until the previous year. To support the Gendarmerie in patrolling the border, the nascent Austrian Armed Forces (whose first recruits had only reported to their barracks in mid-October) sent hastily assembled 'alarm formations' to the border. Strict orders were given to shoot if armed soldiers, including Soviets, refused to surrender their arms; and in November a Soviet soldier who pursued refugees onto Austrian territory was actually killed.

With the second Soviet intervention, fears arose that 'they might come again'; in addition, Czechoslovak troop movements led to fears of a simultaneous attack from the north. The Austrian Army took up defensive positions further back from the border on 5 November. The main task remained to assist police, gendarmes and non-governmental organizations to care for the refugees, however. Western commentators – many of whom had been rather sceptical about Austria's new-found neutrality in 1955 – praised Austria's firm pro-Western stand in 1956. James Michener, sent by the US government to report on the plight of the refugees, wrote in his book *The Bridge at Andau* that 'it would require another book to describe in detail Austria's contribution to freedom. I can express it briefly only in this way: If I am ever required to be a

Although precise figures are difficult to obtain, it is estimated that some 3,000 Hungarians and 720 Soviet soldiers were killed in the street battles. During heavy fighting many insurgents and civilian victims were buried close to where they fell; their bodies were later reburied in cemeteries. (Hungarian Military Museum)

refugee, I hope I make it to Austria.' A country which had regained its sovereignty only a year before, and an army only a few weeks old, had passed this test with flying colours.

Soviet propaganda accused Austria, the Red Cross and other organizations of supporting the uprising by smuggling in arms. Although some weapons were actually brought in, the majority of arms used in the uprising came from Hungarian sources. Many Austrians supported the Hungarians' fight for freedom by other means, however: Austrian students and Boy Scouts crossed the border and travelled as far as Budapest to bring in medical supplies.

Altogether, about 180,000 refugees came to Austria in the autumn and winter of 1956–57. Most eventually moved on to other countries, while some returned to Hungary, but 35,000 were accommodated in

For thousands of Hungarians, the bridge at Andau became their passage to freedom. It was eventually destroyed by Hungarian and Soviet forces on 22 November. The picture shows a group of refugees on the partially destroyed bridge. (Austrian Army/HBF)

Austria. The loss of these refugees – including some of the best and the brightest – was only the most recent in a series of 'brain drains' from Hungary, following the escape to the West of many Jews (including leading nuclear scientists) in the 1930s, and of many conservatives and bourgeois Hungarians after 1945.

Among those who retreated over the border was the former commandant of the military academy, Béla Kiraly, who had been discharged and sent to jail in the purges of the early 1950s, and who was appointed commander of the new National Guard in 1956; he eventually became a professor of history in New York.

Aftermath

After the fighting stopped 'normalization' in Hungary returned only slowly. On 21 November 1956, Soviet forces prevented the assembly of the Central Workers' Council, thus assuring the authority of the new Kádár government. On the same day, following guarantees of safe passage, Imre Nagy and his followers left the Yugoslav Embassy where they had found refuge; they were promptly arrested, and were eventually interned in Romania.

However, political opposition continued, and it was months before the new regime felt secure. On 2 December the Central Committee of the renamed 'Socialist Workers' Party' formally declared the events of October to have been a 'counter-revolution' based on four pillars: the mistakes made under Rákosi, the anti-Party agitation of Nagy and his group, the internal 'Horthy fascists' and other 'capitalist-feudalist' groups, and the involvement of 'international imperialism'. These latter charges were flagrant lies, but provided a pretext for the ensuing repression. Kádár did not formally re-create the hated secret police, but in November 1956 three officers' regiments *(Forradalmi Tiszti Ezredek)* were formed from Army officers, former secret policemen and Communist Party functionaries; these were commonly known as 'Kádár Hussars', or 'Padded Jackets' after their garments. Mass arrests started in December, and martial law was reintroduced. On 8 December more than 100 people died when shooting broke out in Salgótarján. When strikes continued, the workers' councils were outlawed on 12 December 1956.

Throughout 1957 the repression continued. To replace the 'Kádár Hussars' a voluntary workers' militia was established in February 1957, consisting of reliable supporters of the regime. Altogether, not counting short-term arrests, some 33,000 people are estimated to have been imprisoned or sent to internment camps, and some 230 were executed. State Security worked hard to identify participants in the uprising – some of the pictures in this book come from their archives. In some cases, participants were only identified and imprisoned years afterwards, when they were identified from photographs published in foreign journals.

Imre Nagy and his followers were eventually put on trial in 1958. Nagy, Pál Maléter and Miklós Gimes were executed for 'treason and overthrowing the legitimate order', while others received long prison terms. It was obviously intended that this trial be publicized, and a documentary film was made at the time. It was never released in full before 1989, however, as the 'leaders of the counter-revolution' actually appeared in the footage to be sincere, honest people. (The film was later shown in the House of Terror Museum in Budapest, which opened in 2002.)

The suppression of the Hungarian Revolution, the Soviet interventions and the brutal repression that followed led to a major crisis of Communist credibility in the West. Most Communist parties in Western countries lost huge numbers of their members, and eventually lost their influence in politics; those leaders who stubbornly clung to the Stalinist line lost all credibility. If anything, the divide between East and West was consolidated by events in Hungary.

'Goulash Communism', and the end of the Iron Curtain

From mid-1957, Kádár felt safe enough in power to introduce a series of economic reforms that helped to improve daily life for the general population. He understood that for the majority a decent standard of living was more important than political issues. On 10 November 1956 the first pay increases and tax reforms had already been announced. Carefully paced reforms led to what was known eventually as 'goulash Communism', Hungary becoming 'the merriest barrack in the Soviet prison camp'. Internment camps were finally closed in 1961, and in 1963 a general amnesty was proclaimed. Still, those who had participated in the Revolution continued to face difficulties; they were refused passports to travel to the West, and their children were excluded from advanced education. Even in 1989 some 8,000 informers were still active, with 165,000 Hungarians under observation by the security service.

Only from the mid-1980s was it possible to discuss the events of 1956 more openly. Partly because of worsening economic conditions, there was a rift within the Party between conservatives and reformers. The position of the latter was helped by Mikhail S.Gorbachev's reform programme in the Soviet Union, and the 'democratic opposition' in the Hungarian Party gained strength. Kádár was eventually obliged to resign in May 1988; in the same year, a historians' commission was formed to investigate what had happened in 1956. The events of 1956, long denounced as a 'counter-revolution', were now acknowledged to have been a 'popular uprising'. On 16 June 1989, 31 years after their execution, the remains of Imre Nagy and four other victims once buried in unmarked graves were re-interred in Heroes' Square; more than 200,000 people attended the ceremony. Kádár died soon afterwards, by a strange coincidence on the very day that Nagy was officially rehabilitated by the supreme court.

That summer, East German refugees started to cross the border between Hungary and Austria; and at a 'picnic' organized by the Hungarian Democratic Forum and the Pan-European Movement on 19 August, right on the border near Sopron, hundreds of East Germans made a mass crossing. Three weeks later, on 10 September, the border was officially opened. Thus Hungary, in 1956 the tensest sector of the Iron Curtain, became the site of its collapse 33 years later. On 23 October 1989 the People's Republic became a real democratic republic; in 1990 the first democratic elections were held; and in May 2004 Hungary joined the European Union. With the coming implementation of the Schengen agreements by Hungary in 2007, the border which has for so long been a symbol of a world divided will be gone for good.

THE OPPOSING FORCES

THE HUNGARIAN ARMY IN 1956

Following the signing of the armistice ending the country's participation in the World War II Axis, a new Hungarian Army was formed on 20 January 1945. This force operated under Soviet command during the final phases of the war, while other Hungarian units were still fighting alongside the *Wehrmacht*. As in the political arena, Communist control of the military tightened over the years. Because of Stalin's fears of an impending attack by the West, the forces of Eastern countries were increased, putting additional strains on already weak economies. The Hungarian People's Army grew from 36,000 in 1948 to over 211,000 in 1952, with almost 33,000 officers. The aim was a standing force of 12 divisions, with a mobilized strength of 20 divisions. This was never achieved, however, and after 1953 the Army was again reduced, to 140,000 men by 1956. This reduction, and frequent political 'cleansings', cost a large number of officers (both active and reserve) their commissions. In 1956 many of these provided trained personnel for the revolutionaries.

(continued on page 41)

INSURGENTS, EVENING 23 OCTOBER 1956
1: Student
2: Police Corporal
3: Worker

A

B

INSURGENTS, LATE OCTOBER/ EARLY NOVEMBER
1: Béláné Havrilla
2: János Mesz
3: Tibor Fejes József

INSURGENTS, LATE OCTOBER/ EARLY NOVEMBER
1: Artillery Lieutenant, Hungarian Army
2: Youth with Molotov cocktail
3: Nurse
4: Wounded insurgent

D

HUNGARIAN ARMY, 1951–56
1 & 4: Lance-corporal, Infantry
2: Colonel, Armoured Troops
3: Major, Artillery – political leader

HUNGARIAN SOLDIERS SUPPORTING THE REVOLUTION

1: Corporal, Infantry
2: MajGen Pál Maléter
3: Captain, Infantry

E

SOVIET FORCES, BUDAPEST
1: Col Y.I.Malashenko, C-o-S, Soviet Special Corps
2: Major, Artillery
3: Corporal, Airborne Troops

F

THE END OF THE REVOLUTION
1: Lieutenant, Hungarian ÁVH
2: Senior Lieutenant, Soviet MVD
3: Hungarian 'Kádár hussar'

G

THE AUSTRIAN BORDER
1: Sergeant, Infantry, Austrian Army
2: Hungarian student from Sopron
3: Austrian *Gendarme*

Hungarian Army tanks supporting the Revolution were quickly re-marked, the historic coat-of-arms replacing the red star. Apart from a national flag this T-34/85 crew fly a battalion or regimental colour. The commander wears the dark grey padded helmet of Soviet design, with the tank crew version of the khaki padded jacket – note the red-white-green brassard on his left arm. (MTI Budapest, No.MU1956 1103026)

Hungarian People's Army Order of Battle, October 1956

Under direct Ministry of Defence control
8th Rifle Division (HQ Békéscsaba)
30th Artillery Div (Cegléd)

Air Force & Air Defence Command (Budapest)
26th Fighter Div (Taszár)
66th Fighter Div (Kecskemét)
15th Air Defence Div (Veszprém)
46th AD Div (Budapest)
55th AD Div (Budapest)
58th AD Div (Miskolc)

4th Army (Budapest)
3rd Corps (Kecskemét):
27th Rifle Div (Kiskunfélegyháza)
17th Rifle Div (Kaposvár)
5th Mech Div (Kecskemét)

6th Corps (Székesfehérvár):
32nd Rifle Div (Pápa)
9th Rifle Div (Keszthely)
7th Mech Div (Esztergom)

The Hungarian People's Army in 1956 was in a process of reorganization. It included 14 rifle regiments, 6 mechanized rifle regiments, 6 tank regiments, 13 artillery regiments, 6 assault gun regiments, one mortar regiment, one anti-tank regiment, 14 air defence regiments, and support units. Most of its weapons and equipment were of World War II vintage, some of them coming from Soviet stocks; common small arms were the Russian 7.62mm Mosin-Nagant rifles and PPSh sub-machine guns. The main battle tank was still the T-34 armed with an 85mm gun. In the Air Force there were 6 fighter regiments (wings), some already equipped with MiG-15 jets, some still with Yak-9 piston-engined fighters or in transition to the jets.

The involvement of the Hungarian Army and Police in the events of 1956 is difficult to assess in detail. Some units followed orders to resist the insurgents, while others (and individuals) sided with the demonstrators. Street fighting is always difficult, and was especially so for a 'People's Army' ordered to 'liberate' the capital from its own population. It is probably correct to assume that at least half of the armed forces supported the Revolution of 1956. Many soldiers who had been sent on leave because of the restructuring joined the demonstrations in October; tanks and aircraft proudly displayed the new national insignia in place of the red star. In the House of Terror Museum in Budapest there is an example of a regimental colour with the central Communist coat-of-arms cut out.

As the Revolution took on an increasingly nationalist character the Soviet-style uniforms were 'Magyarized' by removing the Russian-type shoulder boards and putting badges of rank on the collar patches, in keeping with the Austro-Hungarian tradition. Red stars and other Communist insignia were removed and – where possible – replaced by

Although the photo is unclear, this young Hungarian Army officer seems to be just about to remove a Red Star badge from his tunic. His cap still bears the Communist coat-of-arms badge on the front of the crown, showing a red star above a hammer and cornstalk, over a riband in national colours – see commentary to Plate D2. (Hungarian Military Museum)

the old Hungarian coat-of-arms. Because of the lynchings of ÁVH personnel, who wore Army-style uniforms with bright blue distinctions, many personnel of the Air Force and signal troops, who also had blue facings (albeit of a different shade), removed their collar patches to avoid being mistaken for State Security policemen.

At least 185 soldiers were killed and 137 wounded during the fighting. Following the crushing of the Revolution the Army was thoroughly combed out; 570 soldiers were sentenced for participating in the Revolution, and 30 were executed. To stabilize the situation and regain control of the officer corps, three regiments (the *Forradalmi Tiszti Ezredek* already mentioned) were formed entirely from officers, former ÁVH and Party personnel. The Kádár regime carefully avoided returning to the old Stalinist symbols, however, and intentionally retained many of the uniform changes effected during the Revolution.

Two insurgents from the Széna Square group, armed with PPSh-41 and Danuvia sub-machine guns; they belong to a party guarding the villa of the former Communist leader Rákosi at Lóránd utca 2 in Buda. Note the variety of clothing worn, including items of military uniform. (Hungarian State Security Archives ÁBTL 4.1, album A-236/ 52)

THE INSURGENTS

The majority of the roughly 15,000 active insurgents were young workers or industrial apprentices from the suburbs, who had in common a disadvantaged background. The very workers whom the Rákosi regime purported to represent were its most enraged enemies due to the low wages, the never-ending vexations of 'working norms', and invented 'subversive incidents' in the factories. Most of them took up arms against the Soviets to overthrow the regime and regain national sovereignty; but there were also some adventure-seekers who joined the insurgents simply in order to get a weapon or exploit the opportunities that might arise later. Soldiers and policemen, writers and other intellectuals, white-collar workers and students also fought in the insurgent ranks, but they were in a minority.

The insurgent groups were formed spontaneously without prior planning or central organization. Western intelligence agencies and the pre-1956 Hungarian émigré organizations remained detached from events before, during and after the Revolution, playing no role in the groups' development or activity. The cores of the insurgent groups were sometimes friends or fellow workers, but in most cases groups formed spontaneously around a dominant, charismatic personality. Normally, groups were known by the name of the major street or square where they fought. The origin, religion or previous political conviction of insurgents played no part. For instance, István Angyal, the joint commander of the Tűzoltó Street group, was a Stakhanovite worker of Jewish origin; while András Kovács, leader of the group from the offices of the Communist daily *Szabad Nép*, had fought as a member of the Arrow-Cross Vannay Battalion in the 1944–45 siege of Budapest.

Neither were the insurgent groups organized on the basis of wider links. The first demonstrators were mainly students, joined later by officials, soldiers on leave and workers. This is clearly evident in the photographs: the demonstrators of 23 October were usually neatly dressed, with jackets and ties worn under the ubiquitous trench coats. (Hungarians always had a reputation for sartorial elegance, but the deprivations of World War II and ten years of Communist dictatorship had taken their toll. Quality and supply had deteriorated, and garments were more and more unfashionable and uniformly made.)

When the students were joined by workers, more varied forms of dress became evident – some examples are shown in the Plates. Most fighters actually came from working-class or rural peasant backgrounds. When Police and Army depots were raided many insurgents acquired items of military uniform, including Soviet-style padded jackets, which were useful in the increasingly cold weather. In the Austrian Police files there is a report of a refugee suspected of being an ÁVH informer because he wore grey-green breeches, which he claimed to have received while fighting with the Corvin group. Partly because of the patriotic nature of the first demonstrations, the Hungarian colours (red-white-green) soon appeared as armbands or lapel ribbons. The general symbol of the Revolution became the national flag with the Communist central motif cut out, leaving a hole.

One of the most remarkable features of the Revolution was the participation of mere boys – not only teenagers, but some as young as eight years old. Accounts, confirmed by Western journalists, speak of them sometimes bravely – or foolhardily – attacking Soviet tanks when the older men wisely retreated. Note the youth of the two boys – probably apprentices from Budapest factories – seen flanking the older man in this photograph. The central figure has a holstered pistol, and an M-48 'Vécsey' stick grenade, its black head painted with three red stripes. (Hungarian National Museum No.69-2295)

The insurgents engaged the Soviets with confiscated Hungarian forces small arms: TT pistols, Mosin-Nagant rifles, PPSh and Danuvia sub-machine guns, hand- and anti-tank grenades, Maxim and Degtyarev heavy and light machine guns, as well as some new AK-47 assault rifles (with wooden or folding stocks) captured from Soviet troops in the early engagements. Although a few weapons were smuggled in from the West, the great majority of those used by the insurgents came from Hungarian sources. Some had small-calibre sporting rifles such as the Levente 5.62mm, which they had taken from the MÖHOSZ, a military sports organization sponsored by the Communist Party. Some early demonstrators obtained weapons from the soldiers sent against them, of whom some surrendered their weapons voluntarily, some after nominal threats; these were mainly pistols, grenades and PPSh sub-machine guns. The workers knew which Budapest factories manufactured and stored arms; those confiscated were mostly Mosin-Nagant rifles, but also Danuvia M-3 sub-machine guns manufactured for the Police. A quantity of weapons and ammunition were taken from ÁVH personnel, mostly pistols and sub-machine guns.

Tactics

The insurgents also had a few T-34 tanks, ISU-152 self-propelled guns, 37mm and 57mm anti-aircraft and 76.2mm anti-tank guns, and BTR-40 armoured personnel carriers captured from the Soviets during the first intervention; but their principal weapon against the Soviet vehicles remained the Molotov cocktail. This was made from any commonplace glass bottle filled with gasoline, and plugged with a rag, which was set on fire before throwing. The insurgents tried to throw the bottles at the air intake grilles on the rear decks of tanks and self-propelled guns, and into the open fighting compartments of armoured personnel carriers. When the bottle hit the target, bullets were sprayed at the vehicle to make sure the sparks ignited the gasoline. Ignition was also made easier by the tendency of Soviet tank engines to overheat when moving slowly, with frequent stops, through city streets. With luck, the fire spread to the fighting compartment and detonated the stored ammunition, destroying the vehicle. Wheeled vehicles where immobilized when the

In a street showing war damage, an Army corporal discusses events with Budapest civilians; see Plate E1 commentary for details of typical insignia changes. The T-34/85 crew fly a large Hungarian flag – since both sides used this type, instant identification was crucial. (Lessing Collection No.56-09-12/ 35A)

From behind the cover of an abandoned Soviet BTR-152, a Hungarian fighter aims a 5.62mm Levente sporting rifle – possibly at ÁVH snipers hiding in apartments opposite. The Levente was a youth organization dating from the Horthy period, and many of its weapons were later used by Communist youth and sports associations. (Hungarian State Security Archives ÁBTL 4.1, album A-237/237)

tyres caught fire. When possible, the insurgents would try to destroy the first and last vehicles in a column, thereby immobilizing the rest. On 25 October an artillery column from the 33rd Guards Mechanized Division was destroyed in this fashion in Ferenc Boulevard, having entered the city without reconnaissance or cover.

Besides Molotov cocktails, some insurgents also used oxygen cylinders or bottles of nitroglycerine obtained from factories and laboratories. According to some sources, on 28 October bottles of nitroglycerine were used to destroy two T-54 tanks at the corner of Kilián Barracks, providing a perfect image for many Western photo-journalists.

Surprisingly, the majority of the insurgents had no military experience; most were too young to have served in World War II or to have been conscripted into the Hungarian People's Army. At best, they had learned basic military skills through the Communist Youth Organization. One older participant who had served in World War II recounted how he and others like him started to instruct the students and workers in the rudiments of handling rifles – explaining, for example, that it was unwise to fumble around with them while pointing them at their friends …

Padded jackets from Army stores appear to have been very popular among the insurgents as the weather became colder. This fighter – who has been lucky enough to acquire a folding-stock AK-47 – wears one along with a civilian beret and scarf. (Hungarian State Security Archives ÁBTL 4.1, album A-236/006)

Unlike Yugoslavia, for instance, Hungary had no tradition of active partisan resistance to invaders; but ironically, many insurgents appear to have profited from watching Soviet propaganda films featuring wartime partisans fearlessly stalking German Panzers, such as Fridrich Ermler's *She Defends the Motherland*, or Sergey Gerasimov's *Young Guard*. Some also took inspiration from the defenders of Stalingrad – before his execution, István Angyal explicitly mentioned this example. These movie role models may also explain some of the photographs that went around the world in October 1956, of young boys posing proudly with hand grenades and Molotov cocktails.

In modern language, this was 'asymmetrical' warfare at its best, with the insurgents skilfully compensating for their disadvantages (small numbers, lack of sophisticated equipment) by hiding in the upper floors of apartment buildings, laying ambushes, and luring tanks into narrow streets where they could be attacked from behind. Against the Soviets' massive technical superiority, the insurgents' tactics at first proved an effective defence, keeping the armed struggle alive until a political solution favourable to them could be achieved. For this reason they did not even attempt to attack the Soviet bases or assembly areas, but only repelled attacks on their own positions, or reconnaissance units trying to locate them.

Their battle positions were usually set up on the third to fifth floors or the roofs of apartment blocks, affording an effective field of fire at Soviet vehicles passing through the main streets. As tanks and personnel carriers tried to speed out of range of the ambushers' bullets and Molotov cocktails, the insurgents used all possible means to slow them down or make them stop. Tram rails and paving stones, as well as tramcars, buses and train carriages were used to erect barricades on the Grand Boulevard, Baross Square, Móricz Zsigmond Square and Széna Square. Elsewhere large amounts of liquid soap or oil were poured over the road to make the tank tracks slip, as in Csepel and Széna Square. The most economical ruse was the fake mine: in the 9th District, soup bowls and pancake pans (sometimes painted green) were laid in rows on the road to resemble anti-tank mines. In order to locate the hidden and dispersed groups, Soviet reconnaissance vehicles tried to use the 'cavalry method': sending a vehicle in at speed, and waiting to see from where it drew fire.

Providing an almost surreal contrast between her old bolt-action M91/30 rifle and the massive ISU-152s knocked out by her group, this blonde girl appears in several photos of the Corvin Passage fighters. She wears a dark civilian overcoat, possibly with a red-white-green ribbon on the left lapel. (Hungarian State Security Archives ÁBTL 4.1, album A-237/195)

Local groups

Of the insurgent groups, the legendary Corvin Passage group was the most effective combat unit at the time of the first Soviet intervention; their headquarters, the Corvin Cinema, can rightly be considered the centre of the armed uprising. Consisting at first of some 40 people, it later swelled to 1,200, led first by László Iván Kovács and then by Gergely Pongrácz. It played a crucial role in halting the first Soviet advance, thus securing the Revolution's brief victory at the end of October.

Although the Corvin Passage group fiercely resisted the second Soviet intervention, their effectiveness could not measure up to their earlier successes due to the now overwhelming Soviet superiority, and also to internal problems. Shelled and mortared before the Soviet infantry advanced, and thereafter stalked by snipers, the pockets of resistance were quickly overpowered, and there was little hand-to-hand fighting. Few insurgents were taken prisoner by the Soviet military; they were usually rounded up later by ÁVH, Police and Soviet MVD units.

The other insurgent units near the Corvin Passage – the Práter Street group, led by János O.Nagy; the Kisfaludy Street groups, led by János Kasza and György Fáncsik; and the Vajdahunyad Street group, led by Károly Kiss and Attila Jánoki – also played a major role in the fighting. Although they acted independently, they frequently fought alongside the Corvin Passage group. Like that unit, they were soon forced to give up the struggle when the second intervention took place.

In the 9th District two groups fought between 24 and 29 October. The Göndör group, led by István Wágner, and the Tompa-Ráday Street group, led by János Bárány, both engaged not only Soviet troops but also Hungarian Army and Police units on several occasions. The Tűzoltó Street group, led by István Angyal and Per Olaf Csongovai, was formed during the ceasefire; it included more than 20 ÁVH conscripts who had switched over to join the insurgents after being detained. At the time of the second intervention these groups resisted the Soviets until 8 November. During the first Soviet invasion the Baross Square group, led by Gyula and Sándor Pásztor and then by László Nickelsburg, conducted lively propaganda activity in addition to fighting. In the second intervention their resistance collapsed almost immediately.

Across the river in Buda, the Széna Square group led by János Szabó was the most important, but compared with other groups their armed resistance to both Soviet interventions was insignificant. However, the Móricz Zsigmond Square group led by Jenő Oláh fought a fierce battle against Soviet troops on 5 November. At this time the insurgents were also supported by a Hungarian Army self-propelled gun unit.

In the outer districts of the city there was intense fighting, mainly during the second Soviet invasion. The Csepel group, led by István Buri and Károly Szente; the Újpest group, led by Sándor Somlyói Nagy; and the Pesterzsébet group, led by László Oltványi, co-operated with various Hungarian military units, and inflicted serious losses on the Soviets with their heavy weapons. The last-named of these groups was that which held out longest in Budapest, resisting until 11 November.

THE SOVIET FORCES

For the Soviet Army, Hungary was never the most important of the empire's garrisons. Soviet war planning echoed that of the Western powers, anticipating the focus of a future conflict in Europe to be further north, in the Soviet zone of Germany and on the north German plains. Hungary was a possible jumping-off point for secondary attacks through Austria, up the River Danube into southern Germany, or into northern Italy via south-eastern Austria or through Slovenia.

Officially there were some 25,000 Soviet troops stationed on Hungarian soil in the autumn of 1956, but the real figures were probably higher. As in most Eastern bloc countries, the Soviet soldiers – mostly conscripts – were normally confined to barracks, and interaction with the civilian populations was deliberately limited. The account of a Hungarian from Miskolc, who belonged to the local council, shows that he and his colleagues learned for the first time which type of unit was stationed there when they entered negotiations with the local commander in late October 1956. In 1955 most of the 40,000 Soviet troops stationed in Austria as the Central Army Group had been withdrawn to garrisons in Hungary, Romania or the western Soviet military districts, in what is now Ukraine.

Units in Hungary were grouped as the army-size Special Corps under direct command from Moscow (reputedly, the name was suggested by Marshal Zhukov himself). Lieutenant-General Piotr N.Lashchenko had his headquarters in Székesfehérvár, commanding two Guards Mechanized Divisions: the 17th in Szombathely in the west, and the 2nd in Kecskemet in the east. (The 'Guards' title denoted elite status earned in World War II; such formations enjoyed better equipment and higher pay. Lashchenko himself had commanded a division during the war, and had been named a Hero of the Soviet Union for his role in the July 1944 offensive by the 1st Ukrainian Front.) These were supported by the 195th Fighter Division and 172nd Bomber Division of the Soviet Air Force.

Apart from their AK-47 assault rifles, these Soviet soldiers photographed in 1956 are wearing almost identical uniforms and equipment to those used during the Great Patriotic War ten years previously. Note the unusual mounting for the rifle in the foreground. (Photo Prof Valeri Vartanov)

Flanked by two staff officers, Col Y.I.Malashenko was the acting chief-of-staff of the Soviet Special Corps in Hungary in 1956. He is seen here wearing the *kitel*, which like most Soviet uniforms still conformed basically to the 1943 regulations – see Plate F1. (Hungarian Military Museum)

Contingency planning for an internal deployment in case of trouble had begun during the summer, and the plan for this Operation *Volna* ('Wave') was agreed on 20 July. On receipt of the codeword 'Compass', the 17th Guards Mech Div was to move to guard the border with Austria, while the 2nd Guards Mech Div concentrated close to Budapest.

On 24 October, two regiments of the 2nd Div – 37th Tank and 4th Mech Rifle – entered Budapest and occupied bridges and railway stations; these were followed by other units. They were not combat-ready, however, and their initial advance was intended simply as an intimidating show of force. Units were not up to full strength, and lacked the strong infantry support essential for mechanized units in urban fighting. Even at full strength a Soviet mechanized division had only two infantry battalions – quite inadequate for street fighting. Soviet units were also hampered by problems of communication and orientation. Tactical radios did not work well in built-up areas – quite often, the Budapest Operational Group HQ had to use civilian telephone lines to communicate with units; and the Soviets lacked good street maps of Budapest.

In addition to the above, two divisions from the Carpathian region – 39th Guards Mech Div and 128th Guards Rifle Div – advanced into Hungary on 24 October, as did the 33rd Guards Mech Div from the Central Group in Romania. The first regiments from these formations – the 407th Artillery and 315th Rifle – arrived in the vicinity of the capital before noon, and were promptly ordered to reinforce troops already in the city. They were soon followed by the 975th Air Defence Regt, while 54th Bridgelaying Regt started construction of a pontoon bridge at Szolnok near Budapest.

Altogether, some 6,000 Soviet troops were in Budapest by nightfall on 24 October, with 290 tanks, 120 armoured personnel carriers, and 156 guns. This was later significantly increased, and during the fighting of the first intervention phase the total reached about 20,000. For the second intervention in November, Hungarian sources give the figures of 31,550 Soviet soldiers, 1,130 tanks or assault guns, 381 other armoured vehicles, 615 artillery pieces or mortars, 185 anti-aircraft guns, and 3,950 trucks, supported by 159 fighter and 122 bomber aircraft. By that time the forces in Budapest had been reinforced by seven regiments (three parachute infantry, two rifle, one tank and one artillery), plus three additional mortar and rocket-launcher units.

In general, Soviet forces had more modern arms and equipment than the Hungarians, including the Kalashnikov AK-47 assault rifle, but also still used older weapons like the Simonov SKS semi-automatic carbine of 1945. Tanks included modern T-54s (with 100mm guns) and lighter PT-76 amphibious models, alongside older T-34s and T-44s (85mm guns), as well as some Josef Stalin IS-3 tanks (with 122mm guns). Various guns and howitzers, both towed and self-propelled, included SU-85, SU-100 and ISU-152 SPs (the latter mounting 152mm heavy howitzers). As mentioned already, artillery was used in the streets of Budapest, causing significant destruction to buildings. No air strikes were launched during the first intervention, however, and only occasional missions in November – both to keep collateral damage within limits, and to avoid even more negative propaganda.

Because Soviets and Hungarians wore similar uniforms and often used the same types of vehicles, identification was difficult and 'friendly fire' incidents certainly occurred. Hungarian insurgent tanks therefore often displayed prominent red-white-green flags in addition to the coat-of-arms newly painted on the turrets. It was as a result of experience in Hungary in 1956 that Warsaw Pact forces sent into Czechoslovakia in spring 1968 bore white 'invasion stripes' on their vehicles.

A Soviet sergeant of a motor transport unit, identified by the rank stripes on his shoulder straps and the arm-of-service symbol on his collar patches, in discussion with Hungarian civilians. Under his khaki canvas 'working jacket' can be seen the stand collar of his *gymnastiorka*, with the white lining strip showing above it. His features suggest that he belongs to one of the southern ethnic minorities, and the expressions on both sides of this conversation are quite friendly; at least 200 Soviet officers and other ranks later faced disciplinary proceedings for criticizing the actions of their own government. (MTI Budapest, No.MU1956 1030016R)

Soviet Special Corps Order of Battle, October 1956

HQ Soviet Forces Hungary
(Székesfehérvár)
(LtGen P.N.Lashchenko)
Corps Troops:
90th Field Artillery Regt (Hajmáskár)
1043rd Air Defence Regt
1 × bridgelaying regt
1 × reconnaissance bn
1 × technical bn
1 × transport bn
1 × mortar '*divizion*' [2 or 3 btys]
plus support units

17th Guards Mechanized Division
(Szombathely):
(MajGen A.V.Kysniecov)
56th Mech Rifle Regt (Szombathely)
57th Mech Rifle Regt (Győr)
58th Mech Rifle Regt (Körmend)
27th Assault Gun Regt (Sopron)
83rd Tank Regt (Várpalota)

2nd Guards Mech Div (Kecskemét):
(MajGen S.V.Lebediev)
4th Mech Rifle Regt (Székesfehérvár)
5th Mech Rifle Regt (Kecskemét)
6th Mech Rifle Regt (Szolnok)
87th Assault Gun Regt (Cegléd)
37th Tank Regt (Sárbogárd)

Soviet Air Force units:
195th Fighter Div (Veszprém)
172nd Bomber Div (Debrecen)

On 24 October, the Special Corps
was reinforced by three divisions:
From Central Group, Romania:
33rd Guards Mech Div
(BrigGen G.I.Obaturov)
From 3rd Corps, 38th Army,
Carpathian region:
39th Guards Mech Div
128th Guards Rifle Div
(Col N.A.Gorbunov)

For the second intervention on
4 November, these forces were
reinforced under the overall
command of Marshal I.S.Konev, who
arrived on 2 November and set up
his HQ at Szolnok:

Special Corps (HQ Tököl AFB,
Budapest):
(LtGen P.N.Lashchenko)
2nd Guards Mech Div
33rd Guards Mech Div
128th Guards Rifle Div
7th Guards Abn Div

8th Mechanized Army (HQ Debrecen):
(LtGen A.H.Babadjanyan)
11th Mech Div
32nd Mech Div
35th Mech Div
70th Guards Rifle Div
60th AD Div

38th Army (HQ Székesfehérvár):
(LtGen K.U.D.Mamsurov)
17th Mech Div
27th Mech Div
39th Mech Div
61st AD Div
31st Guards Abn Div

1st Guards Railway Bde

In addition to the Soviet Army formations (see accompanying table), the 12th Motorized Unit, a brigade-size formation of the Soviet Ministry for Internal Affairs (MVD), was sent from L'viv in Ukraine to Budapest in November. Some of its sub-units were deployed in Budapest and in other towns, while others were despatched to the Austrian border to prevent refugees crossing to the West or supporters of the Revolution from entering Hungary. The MVD co-operated with the Hungarian ÁVH in rounding up suspects, and finally returned to L'viv in January 1957.

FURTHER READING

The following books are the most helpful for anybody wishing to study the events of 1956 in English or German. Special mention has to be made of the photo-book published in 2006 by Thames & Hudson, containing a number of Erich Lessing's brilliant photographs.

Géza Alfoldy, *Ungarn 1956: Aufstand, Revolution, Freiheitskampf. Vorgetragen am 29. Oktober 1996* (Heidelberg, Winter 1997)

Csaba Békés, Malcolm Byrne & János M.Rainer (eds), *The 1956 Hungarian Revolution: A History in Documents* (Central European University Press, Budapest, 2002)

László Borhi, *Hungary in the Cold War 1945–1956: Between the United States and the Soviet Union* (Central European University Press, Budapest, 2004)

Jan Foitzik (ed), *Entstalinisierungskrise in Ostmitteleuropa 1953–1956: Vom 17. Juni bis zum ungarischen Volksaufstand – Politische, militärische, soziale*

und nationale Dimensionen (Schoningh, Paderborn, 2001)

Jenö Györkei & Miklós Horváth (eds), *1956: Soviet Military Intervention in Hungary* (Central European University Press, Budapest, 1999)

Winfried Heinemann & Norbert Wiggershaus (eds), *Das Internationale Krisenjahr 1956: Polen, Ungarn, Suez* (Beiträge zur Militärgeschichte 48, Munich, Oldenbourg, 1999)

László Kontler, *Millennium in Central Europe: A History of Hungary* (Atlantisz, Budapest, 1999)

Melvin J.Lasky (ed), *The Hungarian Revolution: The White Book – The Story of the October Uprising as Recorded in Documents, Dispatches, Eye-Witness Accounts and World-wide Reactions* (Praeger, New York, 1957)

Erwin A.Schmidl (ed), *Die Ungarnkrise 1956 und Österreich* (Böhlau, Vienna, 2003)

In addition, contemporary press reports, etc, are now widely accessible over the internet. Bob Dent's *Budapest 1956: Locations of Drama* (Budapest; Europa, 2006) is an invaluable guide for visitors.

Of the books published in Hungarian, the 'Military Chronicle of 1956' by Miklós Horváth (*1956 hadikrónikája*, Akadémiai, Budapest, 2003) is especially important. Mention should also be made of the three detailed studies on insurgent groups published by László Eorsi for the 1956 Institute in Budapest (*Corvinisták 1956: A VIII. kerület fegyveres csoportjai* ['The Corvinites 1956: The Armed Groups of the 8th District'], 2001; *Ferencváros 1956: A kerület fegyveres csoportjai* ['Ferencváros 1956: The district's armed groups'], 1997; and *A Széna-tériek, 1956* ['Insurgents of the Széna Square, 1956'], 2004).

In striking contrast to the image on page 53, these Soviet officers surprised by the British photographer Jack Esten on 5 November were obviously not amused – on the first day of the second intervention their mood was jumpy. A major reaches for his pistol (see Plate F2); the tall officer behind him actually rushed forward and tried to snatch the camera, but Esten managed to escape helped by another British reporter, Trevor Philpot. Most of this group wear grey officers' overcoats or khaki 'working jackets' over their uniforms; the tank man at the left wears a black or dark brown leather coat. (Photo Getty Images/Hulton Archive)

PLATE COMMENTARIES

All the figures on these plates have been reconstructed from photographs and original items in the Hungarian Military Museum, State Security archives, National Museum and the House of Terror Museum, all in Budapest, with additional information from Austrian and Russian sources. In these commentaries hyphenated model dates – e.g. M-48, M-51 – indicate specifically Hungarian issue items.

A: INSURGENTS, EVENING 23 OCTOBER 1956

The student demonstrations on 23 October 1956 attracted growing numbers of participants; in the course of that evening the demonstrators acquired weapons from police stations and arms factories, and after news spread that the ÁVH had fired on the crowd outside the Hungarian Radio building they began to overturn tramcars to make barricades.

A1: Student

This figure represents one of the students whose demonstrations started the uprising. He is better dressed than the workers who were prominent among the fighters of the later phases – note the jacket and tie worn beneath his trenchcoat; the coat is still worn open, as it was only later that the weather turned bitterly cold. He has just 'equipped himself' with an Army carbine, but wears no other equipment, nor yet the red-white-green brassard; presumably he carries a few rounds of ammunition in his pockets. The 7.62mm Mosin-Nagant, produced under license, was still the standard Hungarian infantry rifle; this is the shorter M44 carbine version, with side-folding bayonet.

A2: Police Corporal

In the first days of the Revolution the Police tried unsuccessfully to restore order, which often resulted in their being disarmed, while other policemen willingly joined the insurgents. On some occasions, such as the siege of the Budapest Party HQ on 30 October, ÁVH members donned Police uniforms in the (futile) hope of escaping the crowd's revenge; insurgents learnt to check their ID cards. The Hungarian Police wore uniforms of the same cut as the Army's M-51, but in dark 'steel-blue' (also called 'plum-blue'), with brass buttons. Collar patches were dark blue with red edge piping and the brass crossed rifles badge of the infantry. Shoulder boards were blue piped in red, here bearing the two yellow silk stripes of a corporal. He is wearing a dark brown belt with a dark steel double-claw buckle and holster – here empty, as A3 has just relieved him of his M-48 pistol. He wears dark blue breeches and black boots, and his blue cap, lying on the ground, shows the red piping, black artificial leather peak and strap. The cap badge features a large red star on a wreathed oval background, almost identical to the ÁVH badge.

A3: Worker

This man could be a worker who joined the student protesters while returning home in the evening. He has just helped himself to the policeman's pistol – a Hungarian copy of the Russian TT-33 (Tokarev-Tula), designated the M-48. He is wearing a three-quarter-length civilian brown leather jacket (details from an original in the House of Terror Museum) and a floppy civilian cap, and has already acquired a red-white-green brassard. At his feet is the street sign 'LENIN KÖRÚT' (now renamed 'Teréz Körút'); red stars and other symbols of Communism were often torn down by the demonstrators.

B: INSURGENTS, LATE OCTOBER/EARLY NOVEMBER

The Corvin Cinema (corvin = raven – the cinema was so named after the 15th-century king Matthias Corvinus), close to a major street crossing and just opposite Kilián Barracks, became one of the crucial battlegrounds from 24 October onwards. The group was led first by László Iván Kovács, then by Gergely Pongrátz; Kovács was probably the single most important individual of the Budapest uprising, since it was he who turned a group of ad hoc demonstrators into a political entity. Representatives of the Corvin köz (= Passage, alley) group negotiated several times with national political and military leaders during the ceasefire, and also influenced other armed groups in their neighbourhood. Although strong Soviet elements attacked again from the evening of 4 November, the 'Corvinites' managed to hold their positions until the next day, when the Soviets followed up an artillery bombardment with another strong attack. The surrounding buildings were seriously damaged and the cinema caught fire; this forced the group to abandon its base, but some members continued fighting in other parts of the city for several days, while others retreated into the cellars of their buildings until they were crushed by the Soviet forces.

B1: Béláné Havrilla

Béláné Havrilla was born in 1932, one of five children, growing up partly in an orphanage. She worked in a textile factory; married in 1952, but soon divorced; worked as a cleaner, then in a lamp factory. On 24 October she took part in the protests, joining the Corvin group first as a nurse, and later taking up arms herself, usually fighting together with Mária Wittner. On 7 November she managed to escape to Austria, but on the urging of her boyfriend returned in December. She was arrested on 25 July 1957, and executed on 26 February 1959.

Photos show that she equipped herself with a khaki padded jacket (differing slightly from the regulation military model in having no side pockets); large stocks of these jackets were kept at Army depots and they were often worn by insurgents in the increasingly cold weather. Here the jacket is not fastened but closed in 'female' (right over left) style, and held fast by the Sam Browne-type belt; she has added a national armband to the left sleeve. She has a standard Mosin-Nagant M91/30 infantry rifle in addition to a holstered pistol.

B2: János Mesz ('Clubfoot' or 'Wooden-Leg Johnny')

Each revolution has its colourful characters. Despite being occasionally labelled a 'World War II veteran' by the Western press, János Mesz was actually born only in 1931, one of 12 children in a worker's family in Pécs. He spent part of his youth in a home for destitute children, and worked at various times as a gardener, a miner and in a factory. He lost his leg in an accident when run over by a suburban train. In 1956 he joined the 'Corvinites' – according to recollections he introduced himself as an officer (which was not true), but actually proved to be a fine gunner, commanding his group's artillery. He was wounded in the head when his anti-tank gun (or 122mm howitzer – accounts vary) was hit and both his two helpers were killed; several photos show him as here, with a bandaged jaw. On 27 October he saved the lives of two injured Soviet soldiers who were taken prisoner.

Béláné Havrilla (see Plate B1) and Mária Wittner fought in one of the groups near the Corvin Cinema. Mária Wittner, armed with a PPSh-41 and a holstered pistol, seems to be wearing a lightweight blue worker's coat. Wounded in the fighting on 4 November, she managed to escape to Austria, but later returned; she was arrested, and sentenced to death in 1958. She was more fortunate than Havrilla, however; her sentence was commuted to life imprisonment, and she was freed in 1970. In 1990 she was awarded the Grand Cross of the Hungarian Republic. (Hungarian State Security Archives ÁBTL 4.1, album A-236/ 019)

Supporting a multi-party system, the withdrawal of Soviet forces from Hungary, and Hungary's leaving the Warsaw Pact, he was not willing to compromise in any way with the government or the Army. On 4 November he fought bravely, but was soon mortally wounded. (Some sources claim that he was taken to hospital and died only two weeks later.)

Here he wears a khaki Army M-51 uniform jacket without insignia apart from a narrow sleeve band in national colours, trousers of apparently the same shade, and a civilian fedora hat. He armed himself with a Mosin-Nagant M44 carbine and a PPSh-41 sub-machine gun; he also carried stick grenades in a canvas pouch for a PPSh drum magazine, and slung an extra 7.62mm machine gun cartridge belt around his body.

B3: Tibor Fejes József

Among the youngest of the Corvin fighters, he was known – for obvious reasons – as 'Keménykalapos' ('Bowler Hat'). Born in 1934 into a workers' family, he spent his childhood in an orphanage after his parents divorced. While still a child he was transferred to Transylvania to work, spent some time in a correctional home, and only returned to Hungary in January 1956. In October he was with the crowd tearing down the Stalin statue, and was among the first members of the Corvin group. When the fortunes of the Revolution turned, he quickly went home on 5 November. Identified from press photographs, he was arrested in April 1957, and executed on 9 April 1959.

He is shown here wearing typical workers' dress – a mid-blue loose shirt and trousers, with heavy laced boots. Over this he wears a lady's dark grey jacket (note the buttons on the left), and a knitted scarf apparently of sand-coloured wool. When photographed he was well armed with a captured AK-47 assault rifle; on his belt are two leather rifle cartridge pouches – probably he had had a Mosin-Nagant before laying his hands on the Kalashnikov. Slung from his shoulder is a thermos bottle.

In the background, note the flag with the central motif cut out, and the captured 76.2mm anti-tank gun with the traditional coat-of-arms being painted on the gunshield – a scene captured in a photograph of the cinema.

C: INSURGENTS, LATE OCTOBER/EARLY NOVEMBER

Most of the fighting against Soviet tanks took place from inside the buildings. Without accompanying infantry, and slowed down by improvised barricades and other tricks, the Soviet tanks and especially the open-topped APCs were 'sitting ducks' for the insurgents above them. These fighters, reconstructed from contemporary photographs, are shown inside an apartment on one of the major avenues.

C1: Artillery Lieutenant, Hungarian Army

This lieutenant, acting as tactical adviser to a group of fighters, wears the regular M-51 tunic but has removed the Soviet-style shoulder boards. The arm-of-service symbols (the crossed cannons of the artillery) have been removed

wounded. Examining a wounded fighter, she is wearing a white medical coat and a red cross armband, to identify her status, over a blue-grey civilian suit and a shirt and tie.

C4: Wounded insurgent

He wears a short black leather windbreaker jacket and brown corduroy trousers tucked into heavy woollen socks, with black-grey rubber boots. At his feet is the reliable Hungarian-made M-27 copy of the 7.62mm Degtyarev DP light machine gun with its 47-round pan magazine which he was manning before he was hit.

D: HUNGARIAN ARMY, 1951–56

About half of the Hungarian People's Army remained loyal to the Communist regime, sometimes participating in the suppression of the uprising from the very beginning – in one case, Hungarian planes even strafed demonstrators. The T-34/85 tank in the background bears the national turret insignia of a red star on a white disc with a red-white-green border (hated by the troops, for the excellent aiming mark it provided for an enemy gunner).

D1 & D4: Lance-corporal, Infantry, field dress with equipment

Of all the Warsaw Pact forces, the uniforms of the Hungarian People's Army between 1951 and 1956 most closely resembled the Soviet pattern. This figure represents an infantry lance-corporal in field marching order; the green collar patches with brass infantry crossed rifles badge are visible, but his equipment hides the single green rank stripe across his shoulder straps. The Hungarian version of the Soviet *gymnastiorka* shirt-tunic differed in having a fall instead of a standing collar; note the white lining strip sewn inside the collar, and the reinforcements at elbows and knees. Standard Hungarian Army boots were modelled on the Soviet pattern, but with only the feet and ankles made from reinforced leather, the shafts being of rubberized canvas. He wears only two ammunition pouches on the right side of his brown leather belt, although the knapsack straps were designed for a symmetrical arrangement; his weapon is the standard 7.62mm Mosin-Nagant M91/30 rifle. The parade helmet was dark green, with the same painted insignia as on the tank turret; it is worn here strapped to the backpack, while he wears a *pilotka*-style cap with a miniature version of the same badge. A blanket and greatcoat roll is strapped around the knapsack, and a messtin to its back; below this note the rolled tent-half in brown, green and sand camouflage pattern, and the water bottle and entrenching shovel strapped to his belt; a gasmask satchel is slung to his left hip, over the bayonet scabbard. (The water bottle was often carried inside the knapsack.)

D2: Colonel, Armoured Troops

This colonel wears the uniform introduced in 1951 – that most commonly worn in 1956. It differs from the earlier M-49 pattern by having two internal breast pockets only, with external flaps, thus more closely resembling the Soviet *kitel*. Tank troops had black collar patches piped bright red with a gilt tank symbol. In Soviet style, this rank is indicated by two red stripes and three silver stars on the shoulder boards, which are of gold braid on black backing for the technical branches. Armour officers' caps had a black band and red piping, with the standard cap badge on the band rather than the crown. The badge was a light blue oval within a gilt wreath and above a narrow red-white-green riband, the oval bearing a red star above a gilt crossed hammer and cornstalk.

János Mesz (see Plate B2), one of the more remarkable leaders of the Corvin group, poses here in front of the cinema. He was mortally wounded in the second round of fighting early in November; today a wooden memorial to him may be seen on the right side of the cinema. (Lessing Collection No.56-09-11/ 34)

from his red collar patches and replaced with two small gilt rank stars, in the pre-Communist fashion. He has also replaced the Communist coat-of-arms badge on his cap with an improvised strip of cloth in national colours. The PPSh sub-machine gun was license-produced in Hungary, and alongside the Mosin-Nagant rifle was a standard infantry weapon of the Hungarian People's Army. A mid-brown Sam Browne-style belt supports his holstered M-48 pistol.

C2: Youth with Molotov cocktail

This teenager, perhaps an industrial apprentice, is wearing a dark grey beret, which was a common civilian headgear at the time (called a 'Swiss cap' by the Hungarians), and a dark civilian jacket over his collarless shirt. He is shown in the process of igniting the Molotov cocktail which he is about to throw down on a passing Soviet vehicle. Leaning next to him is a Hungarian-made Danuvia M-3 sub-machine gun, an excellent but expensive weapon produced in small quantities in 1953–54 for the Hungarian Police. Like the PPSh, it took a short 7.62mm pistol cartridge.

C3: Nurse

Presumably a medical student from the university, this young woman is representative of the many doctors and nurses who participated in the fighting, some being killed or

The 22-year-old Tibor Fejes József (see Plate B3) was another personality of the Corvin group, nicknamed 'Keménykalapos' for his unusual choice of headgear. The T-34/85 in the background may be one of the five tanks lost during the last-minute Soviet attempt to overcome the Corvin Passage insurgents on 28 October. (Hungarian National Museum No.69-2294)

Officers usually wore a belt of old-fashioned Sam Browne design, with a cross strap (oddly) over the right shoulder, although the pistol holster was worn on the right hip.

D3: Major, Artillery – political leader

This major wears the older M-49 uniform still occasionally seen in the mid-1950s; rather longer than the M-51, it had four pockets, and was slightly reminiscent of the old Austro-Hungarian style. The red collar patches show the crossed cannons of the artillery. Again, the shoulder boards have the two red stripes of field grades, here with one rank star, and on the red backing of this arm of service. Buttons were similar for all uniforms, bearing the Hungarian Communist coat-of-arms; they were made either from pressed yellow metal or from khaki/brown Bakelite. Appointment as a political officer was indicated by a badge on the left sleeve, showing a red star on a red-edged khaki pentangle; political 'leaders' like this officer had an additional small yellow star superimposed. (This badge was officially discontinued in 1952.) The ribbons on his chest include Hungarian and Soviet decorations, and the red star badge on his right breast is a typical souvenir, such as that issued in 1955 commemorating the tenth anniversary of victory over the Germans. Note that the all-khaki cap is unpiped, and the badge is worn on the crown. Some of these political officers were pure Party creatures, but others did a lot for the education of their soldiers.

E: HUNGARIAN SOLDIERS SUPPORTING THE REVOLUTION

A considerable number of officers and other ranks joined the insurgent ranks in October. When the new government came into being, immediate changes in uniform details were evident, most commonly the removal of the Soviet-style shoulder boards, and the display of rank insignia on collar patches in old Austro-Hungarian fashion. Red star badges were removed from the caps and replaced with red-white-green badges or strips of cloth, or improvised badges showing the traditional coat-of-arms. Some soldiers also wore red-white-green armbands, while vehicles prominently displayed the coat-of-arms and red-white-green flags – like the T-34/85 in the background. Its crewman wears a dark grey padded crash helmet of Soviet style, and winter overalls.

E1: Corporal, Infantry

This soldier wears the khaki-brown greatcoat over a *gymnastiorka*, semi-breeches and boots. The greatcoat, directly copied from the Soviet model, was possibly the best-liked piece of Russian equipment: it had no buttons (which got ripped off all the time), but was fastened with four hooks-and-eyes. The plain khaki shoulder straps would have shown his rank (two stripes in green arm-of-service colour), but this has been removed. Instead, rank is now shown by two

It is not clear whether this is a soldier or a civilian insurgent who has got hold of uniform items, but the latter seems more likely. The cockade replacing the Communist coat-of-arms on the khaki Army cap is remarkable; it recalls those of the 1848–49 Hungarian Revolution, and similar cockades are still worn today each 15 M⸱⸱ (Hungarian State Security Archives ÁBTL 4.1, album ⸱ ⸱8/ 255)

This young girl poses proudly with a Molotov cocktail, in front of a Soviet 122mm M1930 field howitzer captured by the Corvin group; note the Hungarian coat-of-arms newly painted on the gunshield. She wears mainly Hungarian Army uniform items – a shirt-tunic, breeches, boots and belt – with a civilian beret, coloured scarf and flashlight. (Hungarian State Security Archives ÁBTL 4.1, album A-236/ 010)

yellow stripes replacing the crossed rifles on the *gymnastiorka* and greatcoat collar patches. His khaki wool flapped winter cap, a copy of the Russian *ushanka* but without the fleece, has had the red-star-in-a-circle badge replaced with an improvisation in national colours; a matching armband also shows his support for the Revolution. He is armed with a PPSh-41, and a canvas pouch for a spare drum magazine (here obscured – see G3) would be looped to his mid-brown leather belt with its steel single-claw buckle.

E2: Major-General Pál Maléter
One of the heroes of the Hungarians' fight for freedom, the newly promoted and appointed defence minister is shown as he appeared during negotiations with the Soviets on 3 November. He wears the khaki-brown double-breasted, rather civilian-looking jacket introduced for Air Force and tank officers following the Soviet 1949 model, as an alternative to the tunic, and worn mainly for parade and walking-out dress. The collar and cuffs are piped red, and the black patches are edged in gold; instead of the tank symbol (see D2) they now

bear the three gilt stars showing his former rank as colonel of tank troops. (Preserved in the National Museum in Budapest, his M-51 tunic likewise has the new collar patches.) Note that although he has removed the Soviet-style shoulder boards, on his right chest he still wears two tiny star badges: a Soviet partisan star of 1944, as well as a red star awarded for successful coal-digging by his regiment at Tatabánya. The Hungarian and Soviet medal ribbons on his chest were retained not only from proper pride but as a reminder to the Soviet negotiators that they had been brothers-in-arms against the Germans; predictably, this did not save him from treacherous arrest and eventual execution.

E3: Captain, Infantry
During the Revolution many officers were said to have been busy looking for old, pre-1951 field caps of traditional Hungarian style. This captain has found one, showing the red-white-green cockade on the front of the high crown, as well as a triangular infantry-green patch on the left side, crossed by three yellow silk braids. Again, his M-51 uniform lacks shoulder boards and has the three stars of his rank added to the collar patches – the arrangement of the stars varied. The officers' greatcoat flung over his shoulders differs from the enlisted men's version, having two rows of four gilt buttons, and infantry-green collar patches with a small gold button at the tip above the arm-of-service badge. He has acquired a Soviet 7.62mm Simonov SKS semi-automatic carbine; entering service in 1945 and still used by the Soviet Army in 1956, it took 7.62 × 39mm ammunition in an integral ten-round magazine and had a folding bayonet.

F: SOVIET FORCES, BUDAPEST
Soviet forces in 1956 still mainly wore the uniforms introduced in 1943, with a shallow standing collar both to the ubiquitous *gymnastiorka* shirt-tunic and the *kitel* tunic.

F1: Colonel Y.I.Malashenko
In 1956 Col (later Gen) Yevgeny Ivanovich Malashenko, then 32 years old, was acting chief-of-staff of the Special Corps in Budapest. He had already commanded troops in the Great Patriotic War, and eventually moved on to various staff positions in the Warsaw Pact. His account of 1956 (published in the book edited by Györkei and Horváth – see 'Further Reading') provides rare insights into how the Soviets experienced these events. He wears the standard olive-khaki officers' *kitel* tunic, which had not changed much since 1943; it has scarlet piping at the collar and cuffs. The 1955 regulations reduced the variety of arm-of-service colours; thereafter most branches wore raspberry-red (though generals retained scarlet; tank, artillery and technical troops, black; and medical corps, green). There is a small gilt wreathed star staff insignia above the three silver rank stars on his gold braid 'everyday' shoulder boards, which have scarlet bases but two raspberry-red stripes. Medal ribbons and an academy badge are worn on his left and right breast respectively. For officers the red cap star had been replaced by a smaller star on an oval backing in 1955, but the old badge was often retained in 1956, and we take the liberty of showing it. For parade and walking-out dress the olive-khaki breeches were replaced with dark blue, piped red at the outseams.

F2: Major, Artillery
This figure is copied from a famous photograph (see page 55) showing a group of officers surprised by a photographer on 5 November. His olive-khaki cap with black peak and strap has red piping to the crown and the black band, and

canvas, lacking the leather reinforcements of the Hungarian boots. He is armed with the AKS folding-stock version of the AK-47 Kalashnikov; it fired the Soviet 7.62 × 39mm round, from 30-round curved box magazines – note the pale canvas pouch for these on his brown leather belt, and its star-design buckle. The famous 'wire-cutter' bayonet for the AK-47 was only introduced in 1959; before that date a more traditional design was used.

In the background, the NCO commander on the T-54 wears the characteristic dark grey canvas padded helmet, and a long black leather jacket over his *gymnastiorka*; no insignia are visible. Besides greatcoats and leather jackets, photographs also show non-regulation three-quarter-length light khaki canvas 'working' jackets, similar in cut to the double-breasted leather jackets, worn with or without insignia by both officers and other ranks. The standard tank turret markings of the period were large white or yellow three-digit numbers, often followed by a geometrical design such as an open diamond shape.

G: THE END OF THE REVOLUTION

The Soviet Army was assisted by Soviet and Hungarian state security personnel during the weeks following the second intervention. This plate shows a Hungarian and a Soviet officer discussing details of an operation, while a member of the newly created 'Kádár Hussars' waits for orders. The BTR-152 troop carrier in the background was the standard APC, produced from 1950; it could carry 17 troops in addition to the driver and co-driver.

G1: Lieutenant, Hungarian ÁVH

Although it was reorganized as the *Allamvédelmi Hatóság* (ÁVH, State Security Authority) in 1950, six years later the Hungarian equivalent of the Soviet NKVD continued to be popularly known – and hated – by its old initials 'ÁVO'. It was officially abolished in late October, but some personnel continued in state service and eventually aided the Soviet forces. Members wore Army uniforms – in this case the M-51 – with bright blue branch colour distinctions, and a cap badge resembling that of the Police, with a prominent red star. The khaki-brown cap has a brown leather peak and strap, bright blue band and crown piping. The bright blue collar patches show crossed rifles like the infantry; the gold braid shoulder boards have bright blue edging and single rank stripe, and two silver rank stars.

It should be noted that the Border Guards also fell under the Ministry of the Interior, and wore a similar uniform but with bright green distinctions. Border Guards, notably sharpshooters, were involved in some of the fighting in Budapest.

G2: Senior Lieutenant, Soviet MVD

In 1946 the *Narodnyi Kommissariat Vnutrennikh Del* (NKVD, People's Commissariat for Internal Affairs – i.e. Stalin's secret police) was renamed the MVD when the people's commissariats became 'ministries'. While the secret service eventually became the KGB in 1954 (downgraded to a 'committee' after the fall of Lavrenty P.Beria), the MVD

the oval-shaped officers' badge introduced in 1955. He wears the officers' grey greatcoat with gilt buttons, and the black collar patches according to the 1955 regulations with the gold crossed cannons branch badge at the top. The colour of the collar patches signified the larger formation (raspberry-red for rifles, black for artillery and technical troops, etc), whereas the symbol represented the speciality: e.g. members of an artillery unit attached to a rifle division therefore wore artillery branch badges on infantry raspberry-red patches. Under his coat the standing collar of his khaki *gymnastiorka* shows the two dull gilt buttons. Note the leather lanyard connecting the butt of his TT-33 pistol to the right side of the belt; belts were brown, but boots black.

F3: Corporal, Airborne Troops

This appearance is typical of the second intervention, with the cold-weather *ushanka* cap in grey cloth and fleece instead of the olive-khaki *pilotka* sidecap. Some of the airborne units of the November intervention came from the Caucasus region, hence this soldier's sallow complexion and dark hair and eyes. He wears the grey-khaki enlisted ranks' greatcoat, without buttons, over his *gymnastiorka*; the collar patches are of infantry raspberry-red with the parachute arm-of-service badge at the top, and the olive-khaki field shoulder straps bear two rank stripes in the same colour – the *desantniki* only reverted to their better-known light blue in 1964. On the left sleeve the 1947 patch for parachute troops is a khaki-green diamond with a yellow winged parachute badge, outlined in raspberry-red (light blue for instructors, scarlet for airborne artillery, black for technical troops).

Below the coat, he would wear his parachutist's qualification badge on the chest of the *gymnastiorka*. Note that Soviet soldiers wore boots of near-black rubberized

continued to be responsible for internal order and repression, including the infamous GULAG (*Glavnoje Upravlenije Ispravitelno-trudovych Lagerej*) labour and detention camps. MVD units were also involved in the crushing of the Hungarian uprising of 1956. This lieutenant (holding the senior of three grades of that rank in the Soviet system) wears the characteristic cap with blue piping around the crown, reminiscent of the old 'blue caps' worn by the MVD until 1954; brick red – displayed here on the band – was the MVD branch colour, whereas the KGB had dark blue. Otherwise, MVD and KGB uniforms closely matched those of the Army. This officer wears the olive-khaki M1943 *kitel* with stand collar, piped brick-red at collar and cuffs. Shoulder boards show gold lace on a brick-red base, and one red stripe with three silver stars. He also wears khaki breeches, black boots, and a holster for the 9mm Makarov PM (*Pistolet Makarova*) adopted by the Soviet forces in 1951. It was an extremely simple weapon with few moving parts, and is considered among the best and most reliable designs of its time.

LEFT **A fine posed portrait of a 'Kádár hussar' from one of the three regiments established in November 1956. See commentary to Plate G3 for details of the uniform, insignia and equipment. (Hungarian Military Museum)**

BELOW **The Austrian side of the Hungarian border – see Plate H. At left is a Customs guard; in the background, using binoculars, a *Gendarme* of the rural police. The three soldiers of the fledgeling Austrian Army – whose first recruits were only inducted in October 1956 – wear non–regulation sheepskin jerkins. (Police Headquarters Burgenland)**

At the same spot where thousands of Hungarian refugees had crossed the border into Austria in 1956, the collapse of the Iron Curtain began 33 years later: on 27 June 1989 the Hungarian and the Austrian foreign ministers, Gyula Horn and Alois Mock, ceremoniously dismantled the first piece of barbed wire fence between their countries. Two months later, hundreds of East Germans who had travelled to Hungary crossed into freedom. Today, this memorial recalls those events; the watchtower in the background is preserved as a reminder of grimmer times. (Photo Erwin A.Schmidl)

G3: Hungarian 'Kádár hussar'

As described in the body text, former ÁVH members, other loyal supporters of the Communist regime, and also Army officers who wanted to stay in the military were enlisted into three special regiments. Popularly known as the 'Kádár Hussars' or 'Padded Jackets' (*pufajkások*), after the Army winter garments they were issued, they generally enjoyed a bad reputation for reprisals against anybody who might have been involved in the Revolution. Nonetheless, they wore traditional-style field caps; the Kádár regime was careful to cultivate nationalist Hungarian sentiments, rather than returning to pre-1956 Soviet-style symbolism. This man wears the red star-in-a-circle badge on the khaki-brown cap, although these were soon replaced with badges showing the red-white-green national colours. His mid-khaki padded jacket shows no insignia; note the smooth khaki collar, pockets and elbow reinforcements. Shown here are the padded trousers with reinforced knees – although most soldiers preferred to wear ordinary breeches instead – tucked into standard Army boots of composite construction. He is armed with a PPSh-41; its canvas magazine pouch and a heavy black truncheon are carried at his belt.

H: THE AUSTRIAN BORDER

Some 180,000 refugees made their way to the Austrian border during the grim days of October and November 1956. The Austrian *Gendarmerie* (rural police) were involved in disarming them, before they were brought to improvised refugee camps, which separated civilians from soldiers and 'fighters'. To reinforce the *Gendarmerie*, and also to guard against possible armed incursions (which might offer a pretext for pursuing forces to cross the border, too), hastily formed 'alarm formations' of the nascent Austrian Armed Forces were deployed to the border.

H1: Sergeant, Infantry, Austrian Army

This NCO wears the new M1956 Austrian Army uniform in field-grey shades (greener for the field cap and tunic than the trousers). The collar patches in arm-of-service colour (here, the green of rifle troops) show silver-grey rank insignia of two stars over a narrow and a broad stripe; the cap displays chevrons of the same proportions, surmounted by the Austrian red-white-red cockade on a gilt button. Against the cold he wears a privately acquired, non-regulation sleeveless sheepskin jerkin, and grey suede leather gloves. This is taken from a photograph, although in November 1956 most personnel wore greatcoats – either field-grey copies of the *Gendarmerie* design (see H3) or olive-drab US Army surplus. His equipment is also US Army wartime webbing issue: a pistol belt with the leather holster for his .45cal M1911A1 Colt pistol, and a two-pocket canvas pouch for the 15-round magazines of his .30cal M1 carbine – the weapon of choice for NCOs and officers. The rank and file were armed with Garand M1 rifles and Browning Automatic Rifles (see page 28). The blue-grey spatterdash gaiters are from old *Gendarmerie* stocks.

H2: Hungarian student from Sopron

In Sopron, western Hungary, students of the Agricultural College fought alongside their teachers before eventually crossing into Austria. This figure wears a black student cap of traditional design, with a bright green band, piping, and oak sprig motif on the crown. He is wearing an olive-brown leather jacket with the red-white-green armband fixed to his left sleeve; brown corduroy knee breeches, thick grey stockings and heavy brown laced shoes. He is handing over a Mosin-Nagant rifle with telescopic sight; this sniper version had a bolt of slightly different design, to allow operation with the telescopic sight fixed.

H3: Austrian *Gendarme*

This *Gendarme* wears the traditional blue-grey ('pike-grey') uniform with red distinctions, which had been reintroduced after 1945. Buttons, and the badges and cords on the cap, are gilt, on red backing where appropriate; note on the left side of the cap a 'flaming grenade' badge. Collar patches, cap piping, trouser seam piping and extensive greatcoat piping are bright red. The cap peak and laced boots are dark brown, the latter worn under blue-grey canvas three-strap anklets. He is armed with an old German 7.92mm Mauser Kar 98k, possibly from French stocks (France continued to manufacture the 98k in 1945). The belt and rifle ammo pouches, and the elaborate patrol case worn slung from his right shoulder, are mid-brown leather.

INDEX

Figures in **bold** refer to illustrations.

aircraft: Hungarian 41
Andau bridge **30**
Angyal, István 43, 48
armoured personnel carriers **16**, **25**,
   47, 61, **G**
artillery and AFVs
   anti-tank guns 57, **B**
   howitzers **14–15**, **49**, 53, **60**
Austria: help for insurgents 27–30, 63
Austrian forces **28**, **62**, 63, **H**
ÁVO/ÁVH
   appearance 61, **G1**
   background 6–7
   as refugees 27
   and the Revolution 10, 11, 18, 20, 22

barricades **21**, 49
Border Guards 18, 61
Budapest
   Communist Party HQ **18**, 22
   Corvin Passage and Cinema **15**, 17–18,
      20, 25, 45, **49**, 50, 56–7, **57–9**, **B**
   Hungarian Radio building 9–10
   Kilián Barracks 17–18
   Lövőház Street **21**
   map **13**
   National Theatre **25**
   Parliament building (Kossuth Square)
      12, 13, **14–15**, 24

casualties 3, 25–6, **29**
councils, revolutionary 20, **20**, 22,
   30, 31
criminals: involvement 16

Debrecen 11

Esztergom 18

flags **8**, 9, **12**, **B**
Free Győr Radio 18

Gerő, Ernő **6**, 8, 9, 11–12, 15
Gyurkó, MajGen Lajos 18

Havrilla, Béláné 56, **57**, **B1**
Horthy, Miklós 4
Horvath, BrigGen Nik **28**
Hungarian Army 32–43, 58–60, **D–E**
   3rd Corps 18
   8th Tank Regt 10
   involvement in the Revolution 12, 13–14,
      17–18, 22, 24, 25, 42–3, 59–60, **E**
   Kádár hussars **26**, 31, 43, **62**, 63, **G3**
   Military Technical Auxiliary Corps 18
   NCOs 58, 59–60, **D1**, **D4**, **E1**
   officers **23**, **42**, 57–8, 58–9, 60, **C1**,
      D2–3, **E2–3**
   soldiers 20, **41**, 48

Hungarian Revolution (1956)
   23 October 9–11
   24–28 October (first Soviet
      intervention) 11–21, 52–3
   29 October–4 November (interlude) 22–3
   4–12 November (second Soviet
      intervention) 23–6, 53
   help from abroad 27–30, **27**, 63
   mopping up **26**, 30–1
   negotiations 19–23, **22–3**
   reasons for 16
Hungary
   under Communists 5–9
   history 3–5
   map **5**
   Nagy tries to withdraw from Warsaw Pact
      22–3
   post-Revolution 31–2
   strategic importance to Soviets 51

insignia
   Austrian 63, **H1**, **H3**
   ÁVO 61, **G1**
   Hungarian Army **42**, 58–9, 60, **D2–3**, **E2**
   insurgents 44, **48**, 56, 57–8, 59–60, **59**,
      A3, **C1**, **E**
   Kádár hussars 63, **G3**
   MVD 62, **G2**
   Police 56, **A2**
   Soviet 53, 60–1, **F**
insurgents 3, **17**, 43–50, **43–9**, 56–8,
   59–60, **A–C**
   local groups 24, 50, 56–7, **57–9**, **B**
Iron Curtain, collapse of 32, **63**

József, Tibor Fejes 'Bowler Hat'
   57, **59**, **B3**

Kádár, János 7, 15, 23–4, 31, 32
Kádár hussars **26**, 31, 43, **62**, 63, **G3**
Kállay, Miklós 4
Kecskemét 18
KGB 15, 61, 62
Khrushchev, Nikita 7, 12, 23
Kiraly, Béla 30
Kovács, András 43
Kovács, László Iván 50, 56
Kossuth, Lajos 4

Lashchenko, LtGen Piotr N. 51
Levente 47

Malashenko, Col Y.I. **52**, 60, **F1**
Maléter, MajGen Pál 18, 23, **23**,
   31, 60, **E2**
Malinin, Gen M.S. **22**
Mesz, János 'Wooden-Leg Johnny' 56–7,
   58, **B2**
Miskolc 18, 51
Mosonmagyaróvár 18
MVD 61–2, **G2**

Nagy, Imre
   before the Revolution 7, 8
   during the Revolution 9, 11, 15, 20, 22, 24
   after the Revolution 30, 31, 32
Nagykanizsa 18
nurses 58, **C3**

Police 56, **A2**
Pongrácz, Gergely 15, **24**, 50

Rajk, László 7, 8
Rákosi, Mátyás **3**, 5–6, **6**, 7
Red Cross **27**, 29
refugees 3, 27–30, **30**, 63, **H2**

Serov, Ivan A. 15, 23
Sopron 63
Soviet forces 51–4, 60–1, **F**
   2nd Guards Mech Div 13, 25, 51, 52
   7th Guards Airborne Div 22, 24
   8th Army 24
   12th Motorized Unit 54
   17th Guards Mech Div 51, 52
   31st Guards Airborne Div 22, 24
   33rd Guards Mech Div **14**, 17, 25, 52
   38th Army 24
   39th Guards Mech Div 52
   128th Guards Rifle Div 17, 25, 52
   172nd Bomber Div 51
   195th Fighter Div 51
   airborne units 61, **F3**
   NCOs 53, 61, **F3**
   officers **22**, **52**, 55, 60–1, **F1–2**
   order of battle 54
   presence in Hungary 11
   soldiers 11, **35**, 51
Stalin, Joseph: toppling of statue 9
students 8–10, **8**, 56, 63, **A1**, **H2**
Suez Canal crisis (1956) 26–7

tanks
   PT-76 **17**
   Soviet **12**, 53
   T-34/85 **18**, 41, **41**, 59, **59**, **E**
   T-54 **10**, **16**, 61, **F**
Tiszakécske 18

United States 27

weapons
   Austrian 63
   carbines
      M1 63, **H1**
      M44 **19**, 56, 57, **A1**, **B2**
      Simonov 60, **E3**
   grenades **26**, 44, 57, **B2**
   Hungarian Army 41
   insurgents 45
   light machine guns 58, **C4**
   Molotov cocktails **45**, 46–7, **60**, **C2**
   pistols 44, 57